Becoming an
Effective Leader

The Results-Driven Manager Series

The Results-Driven Manager series collects timely articles from *Harvard Management Update*, *Harvard Management Communication Letter*, and the *Balanced Scorecard Report* to help senior to middle managers sharpen their skills, increase their effectiveness, and gain a competitive edge. Presented in a concise, accessible format to save managers valuable time, these books offer authoritative insights and techniques for improving job performance and achieving immediate results.

Other books in the series:

A Timesaving Guide

THE RESULTS-DRIVEN MANAGER

Becoming an
Effective Leader

. . .

Harvard Business School Press

Boston, Massachusetts

ISBN-13: 978-1-59139-780-9

Library of Congress Cataloging-in-Publication Data

The Results-driven manager : becoming an effective leader.
        p. cm.—(The results-driven manager series)
    ISBN 1-59139-780-4
  1. Leadership. I. Title: Becoming an effective leader. II. Harvard
Business School. III. Series.
    HD57.7.R468 2005
    658.4′092—dc22   2004022261

Contents

Contents

Starting Out on the Right Foot

Becoming an
Effective Leader

Introduction

· · ·

Congratulations! You've just been promoted to a leader-ship position for the first time. You've celebrated the good news with family and friends, allowed yourself a moment to take pride in your achievement, and in-dulged in visions of wielding your newfound power with wisdom and sagacity. You know that leading a team, department, or unit is almost certainly going to pose all sorts of new challenges, but you feel confident that you'll succeed. Or perhaps you've served in a leadership role for a while and you've decided to strengthen your skills to meet new challenges facing your company.

In either case, you'll need confidence to excel in your efforts. But you'll also need a heavy dose of realism—an accurate understanding of what leaders actually do, how they operate, how they enhance their abilities, and how they achieve the best results for their companies. The nature of leadership is changing, and too many freshly minted *and* more seasoned leaders are operating from outdated assumptions about what the job entails. As a result, they're not getting the best from their people *or* themselves—and their companies are paying the price.

Leadership: An Evolving Notion

There's no getting around it: The nature of leadership has changed. And numerous businesspeople aren't keeping up with the changes. For example, many leaders assume—wrongly—that merely handing down orders to subordinates will generate the payoff their company needs to compete. Not true. In this age of flatter organizational structures and localized decision making, ordering people around doesn't work the way it used to. Sure, people may comply with your demands, but they'll be going through the motions. Despite their obedient behavior, they won't be giving you their genuine commitment. Moreover, acting like a dictator only stifles a workforce's ability to think creatively—something that's essential for today's organizations as they compete. Rather than fostering fresh ideas, bossing people around only spawns fear and surface-level obedience.

These days, leadership isn't about wielding unilateral power. Rather, it's about mobilizing people to face challenges that require new habits, new values or priorities, or new ways of doing business. It's about getting things done through other people—inspiring them to take responsibility and do the work that only they can do. It's about defining a compelling vision—while letting others decide how to make that vision real. And it's about putting the right structures and processes in place so that your people can sharpen their skills and excel in their jobs—and perhaps learn to become leaders themselves.

A leader who hands down orders or tries to solve every problem single-handedly and unilaterally isn't really leading. After all, as one expert put it, solutions don't solve anything unless they "live" in people's behavior. And that means leaders must help others learn how to solve problems and develop solutions.

But along with these evolving ideas of leadership, certain cultural and economic forces are creating conflicting ideas among workers about what makes an ideal leader. For example, as the pace of change accelerates relentlessly, many businesspeople remain trapped in a crisis mind-set, which can foster a desire within employees to look to their leaders to provide all the answers. Moreover, in the United States at least, cultural traditions glorify those who present a heroic, charismatic front; who give clear answers; and who "make things happen." Witness the many "celebrity CEOs" featured on the covers of business magazines and journals. And notice how almost all of these personages are depicted with resolute, all-knowing expressions on their faces and a determined, take-charge stance.

But whether you're a CEO, manager, or team leader, how can you enable your people to achieve great things if you provide all the answers instead of encouraging people to figure them out? If you take responsibility instead of give it? If you tell your employees how to get to the goal instead of defining the end and letting *them* map out the means?

Recent events have only muddied the leadership picture even further. Specifically, in the wake of the bursting of the dot-com bubble, the September 11 terrorist attacks, and a rash of corporate scandals, a cloud of anxiety has settled over the business arena. People want more from their leaders than ever before—and their needs can sometimes seem mutually exclusive. For example, they want reassurance *and* direction, emotional openness *and* unshakeable confidence, ownership of their work *and* solutions handed to them by someone else.

Boosting Your Chances of Success

Few could argue with the statement that the job of a leader has become tougher and more complex than ever. But as someone who's a newcomer to the leadership role, or who wants to improve your skills, you *can* boost your chances of success. And you can navigate the often conflicting demands that you'll encounter as you carry out your responsibilities.

The process requires discipline. First, you need to anticipate and confront the surprising aspects of the job. For instance, many leaders discover, to their astonishment, that charisma alone won't secure their place at the head of a team, department, or division. Many also find it shocking to learn that the best leaders don't "make things happen" themselves; rather, they effect change through other people. By grasping what real leaders do—and what they don't do—you'll stand a far better chance of mastering your new job or enhancing your skills.

Second, if you're new to the leadership role, you'll want to make sure that you start out on the right foot. A novice leader's first thirty days on the job can set the stage for his or her ultimate success or failure. A handful of strategies—such as learning to delegate, taking charge of your own professional development, and building momentum quickly—can help you score early successes that you can build on later.

Third, you have to understand and confront the changing nature of decision making for leaders today. Specifically, as ambiguity and high pressure increasingly define the business landscape, you need to make decisions more quickly—often with insufficient information at hand. The best leaders know how to gain access to a broad spectrum of data and opinions in order to make the wisest choices for their companies.

Finally, don't forget to master the basics of communication. Without finely honed communication skills, no leader can convey his or her company's vision, inspire followers to greatness, or steer an errant division or team back onto the right track.

The articles in this collection offer a wealth of guidelines for preparing for and surmounting the challenges inherent in the leadership role. Here's a quick preview of what you'll learn as you read this volume.

What Leaders Do—and Don't Do

Experts have long debated what defines a leader, but some consensus has emerged in recent decades. This section lays out a set of characteristics and abilities that today's business leader must possess in order to generate results for his or her organization.

In "What You Can Learn from Jack Welch," Harvard Business School Publishing's editor-at-large Walter Kiechel shares leadership lessons from the legendary former General Electric CEO. Welch, for example, contends that the best leaders display "four E's": very high *energy* levels, the ability to *energize* others around common goals, the *edge* to make tough yes-and-no decisions, and the ability to consistently *execute* and deliver on their promises. In addition, talented leaders "put the right people in the right jobs." They develop people through abundant and varied experiences, never letting them rest on their laurels. And they continuously cull their ranks to eliminate poor performers.

Ron Heifetz, director of the Leadership Education Project at Harvard's Kennedy School of Government, explores the theme of what makes a leader in "The Work of a Modern Leader: An Interview with Ron Heifetz." According to Heifetz, leaders motivate people to handle *adaptive challenges*—shifting business realities that require new ways of doing business, new habits, or new values or priorities. Trust is a critical source of leaders' authority in situations involving adaptive challenges, because it enables leaders to hold people's attention to the hard issues. To earn their people's trust, Heifetz writes, leaders must demonstrate *competence* as well as *consistent values*. Building a track record of identifying and dealing with problems and being honest with people about the challenges facing your firm are two activities that can help you acquire these qualities.

In "Why Authority Still Matters," business writer Loren Gary examines additional qualities of effective leaders. A good leader, Gary maintains, has the "ability to enroll his listeners in a shared sense of destiny that [includes] their own hopes and dreams . . . [He] wins the hearts of followers with his sincerity, his passion, and his ability to give voice to a vision roomy enough for others to recognize themselves in it." Skilled leaders also blend authority with latitude. That is, they specify desired outcomes without dictating how people will achieve those outcomes. Gary cites a compelling metaphor: leaders clearly designate the mountain to be climbed, but leave it up to their followers to select the route and the strategies for reaching the top.

This section concludes with "Lead *and* Manage Your Organization with the Balanced Scorecard," by management consultant Robert S. Kaplan. According to Kaplan, organizations need people who both lead (that is, communicate vision and strategy) *and* manage (orchestrate systems that allocate resources effectively and ensure valid reporting and control). The Balanced Scorecard, a strategy-management methodology created by Kaplan and his colleague, David P. Norton, enables organizations to simultaneously lead and manage. How? It helps leaders define high-level strategy, identify the objectives that must be achieved in order to carry out that strategy, and monitor progress on those objectives. Moreover, it encourages leaders to define strategic objectives not only in financial terms but also in terms of needed changes in internal processes, workforce learning and development, and fulfillment of stakeholders' needs.

As Kaplan makes clear, tools such as the Balanced Scorecard can help you engage in five critical leadership activities: (1) translate your company's vision into operational terms, (2) align your team or department behind the corporate strategy, (3) encourage your employees to take responsibility for carrying out the strategy, (4) make strategy implementation a continuous process, and (5) establish new systems for business planning, resource allocation, and reporting of business results.

The Leader as Charismatic Hero: A Vanishing Breed

Not surprisingly, a workforce's desire for charismatic, take-charge leaders can intensify during times of rapid change. Therefore, it's vital for any leader to understand the roots of such desire—and the importance of resisting the temptation to rely on charisma, instead of true leadership skills, to get the job done. The articles in this section address these themes.

In "No Time for Happy Talk," Walter Kiechel lays out the personal qualities required of today's business leaders. Instead of look-at-me charisma and heroics, leaders must be "emotionally available" to followers, including owning up to vulnerabilities and being able to share bad news openly and honestly. They must also be willing to develop leadership skills in people at the periphery of their organization—people who can demonstrate a diversity of perspectives and interpersonal styles.

Loren Gary describes additional valuable leadership qualities in "Power: How Its Meaning in Corporate Life Is Changing." According to Gary, too many business leaders assume that power equals the "capacity to destroy." Instead, it is the "ability to influence others." The best leaders exert their influence most effectively by creating a work climate that encourages people to serve the organization—rather than seeking to acquire power for their own aggrandizement. Such leaders have a managerial style that's more democratic than authoritarian. In addition, they see themselves as having "a duty to others" rather than others having a duty to them.

In "What Should a Leader Be?" business writer John Hintze focuses on the qualities that enable leaders to generate long-term value for their organizations. "Charisma," as affirmed in this article, "[has] been overrated." Effective leaders instead demonstrate other types of characteristics. For example, they constantly raise the bar for themselves, are self-starters, and recognize that every-body contributes to the organization's success. And they leverage team resources as well as show respect for employees. Finally, they make themselves easily accessible throughout their organization. Though such qualities may not make headlines, they enable leaders to create the most value for companies.

Bill George, retired CEO of Medtronic, sheds additional light on these "softer" qualities in "The Call for Authentic Leadership with Bill George." In George's view, "business [needs] more ethically based leadership . . . We have idolized the wrong leaders, associating image with leadership and confusing stock price with corporate value." Instead, we need "authentic leaders" who "have a deep sense of purpose for their leadership and are true to their core values." Such leaders "are people of the highest integrity who are committed to building enduring organizations" and who "see themselves as stewards of the assets they inherit." They transmit their values by communicating the company's mission every day and making decisions consistent with those values.

In his article "In Praise of Pragmatic Leadership," Loren Gary strikes a similar note. He cites Jim Collins's observation that the best leaders are "plow horses, [not] show horses." They effect fundamental change in sustainable ways by defining inspiring standards and demonstrating a modest personal style. Drawing on a different analogy by Collins, Gary writes that "'instead of being high-profile change agents, [good leaders are] a lot like tofu: clearly part of the meal, perhaps even the main source of nutrition, but the spice [is] provided by everyone around them.'"

David Stauffer's article "10 Myths About Post-heroic Leadership—and Why They're Wrong" wraps up this section. Today's business leader, Stauffer maintains, "sees everyone as a leader, . . . views her primary function as the building of a strong team with a common vision and mutual influence, . . . [and] invites other employees to share the responsibilities of managing—thereby producing better decisions and ideas, more learning, and higher morale." But "post-heroic" leaders aren't "soft"; nor do they believe that it's most important for people to "feel good" and to experience little conflict. Stauffer presents and dispels these and numerous other misunderstandings about such leaders.

Starting Out on the Right Foot

If you'll be assuming the role of a leader for the first time, understanding the changing nature of leadership can help you prepare for the job. But you also need to establish successes early on if you want to excel in the long run. The articles in this section lay out several powerful guidelines.

Business writer Lauren Keller Johnson opens the section with "Debriefing Linda A. Hill: Accelerating the New Manager's Start," an interview with Linda A. Hill, Wallace Brett Donham Professor of Business Administration at Harvard Business School. According to Hill, new leaders must quickly master a new identity—transforming themselves from "task doers" to "people developers." They also have to learn how to delegate—something that many find difficult if they've come to the leadership role directly from an individual-contributor position in which they earned praise by "doing everything themselves." The best leaders, Hill adds, also take immediate responsibility for their own professional development, drawing on their own supervisor's experience and wisdom to begin succeeding in their new role.

Loren Gary explores the theme of self-directed leadership development further in "Pulling Yourself Up Through the Ranks." Using aviation giant Boeing as an illustration, Gary offers several suggestions for leaders seeking to sharpen their skills. These include extracting as many lessons as possible from on-the-job experiences rather than relying solely on classroom learning, knowing when to ask for help, and being open to developing different skills as your company changes.

The most successful leaders not only take charge of their own development; they also begin building momentum during their first day on the job, maintains business writer Eric McNulty in "Taking Charge Fast." How? Among other practices, they craft a strategy for on-the-job learning, create a clear line of demarcation between their former role and their new one, and set the right expectations for their boss, peers, and direct reports.

Management author Jennifer McFarland concludes this section with "Succeeding Ms. (Mr.) Wonderful," which examines the special challenges facing leaders who replace beloved predecessors. "Succeeding a much-admired leader can . . . be a minefield of unspoken expectations," McFarland writes. To defuse a potentially incendiary situation, talk with whomever you're replacing *before* your first day on the job to "learn what you need to know to make sound early decisions." Also, "ask the outgoing leader to talk about her legacy, . . . to describe her managerial style, and to evaluate her team." Your goal? To uncover problem areas as well as secrets for handling the personalities in your new environment."

Making the Best Decisions

In addition to getting off to a strong start, leaders need to master the nuances of decision making. As explained in "Three Skills for Today's Leaders," businesspeople must make decisions more rapidly than ever. Why? "Quick, easily available information allows companies (and their competitors) to move with extraordinary speed." Consequently, "leadership teams are hard-pressed to sift information and make decisions with due haste." To keep pace, leaders must: (1) develop a tolerance for ambiguity, (2) constantly reinvent the way their teams operate and generate ideas, and (3) foster mutual understanding of problems among their direct reports.

But even these skills aren't enough to ensure smart decision making. As *Harvard Management Update* editor

Paul Michelman maintains in "What Leaders Allow Themselves to Know," leaders must also access the full spectrum of available opinions and data to make the best choices for their companies. How? Guard against isolation—by talking with people at every level in your organization. Cultivate candor by regularly sharing a meal with groups of employees. And revisit the reasons for a decision before implementing your plan of action—to ensure that you're on the right track.

Psychology professor Robert B. Cialdini examines this theme further in "The Perils of Being the Best and the Brightest." Far too often, Cialdini opines, a leader "fails to ask for input from team members [and] members . . . relinquish problem-solving responsibilities to the leader," failing to provide him or her with vital information needed for a decision. To gain sufficient input from others, leaders need to set up systems that ensure collaborative exchanges. For example, "encourage everyone with a stake in the decision process to make a contribution to it and . . . assure all concerned that each contribution—while perhaps not the deciding factor—will be a factor in the process" and "will be given full attention."

Communicating Effectively

Clearly, smart decision making, along with other responsibilities of leadership, hinges on effective communication. By mastering the art of communication, new and experienced leaders alike can get the information they need from others, convey a compelling vision, and inspire people to excel in the workplace.

In "Language: Churchill's Key to Leadership," consultant Nick Wreden draws lessons about communication from the revered British prime minister's ability to lead his nation during World War II. According to Wreden, Winston Churchill was able to rally the British people to stand up against the Nazi juggernaut by applying just a few simple communication techniques that any leader today can master. These include using precise, economical diction; building on startling facts; using analogies to clarify abstractions; and leavening your delivery with wit and a chuckle.

Business-book reviewer Janice Obuchowski offers additional suggestions for communicating effectively in "Three Keys to Leadership Communication Today." Drawing from Robert Mai's and Alan Akerson's *The Leader as Communicator: Strategies and Tactics to Build Loyalty, Focus Effort, and Spark Creativity*, Obuchowski maintains that effective communicators demonstrate these capacities: (1) they foster trust; for example, by welcoming each new hire and explaining the company's philosophy, (2) they set direction and instigate action by discussing their organization's future with employees and providing them with information to deepen their understanding, and (3) they encourage debate and let employees know that their ideas are valued.

Like all leaders, you will almost certainly find some aspects of your job overwhelming. In today's world of ever-accelerating change and evolving ideas about what defines an effective leader, few individuals transition into the leadership role or hone their abilities without encountering at least some daunting challenges. The articles you're about to read can help you anticipate and confront those challenges, as well as strengthen a handful of essential skills.

To leverage the guidelines and practices offered in this collection, keep these questions in mind as you read:

- How can I best acquire and exert influence in my role as a leader?

- What tools will help me communicate my company's vision and strategy to my people as well as ensure that resources are allocated effectively?

- How might I set up systems and processes that enable my people to excel?

- How will I resist the impulse to provide all the answers and solve all the problems facing my group?

- If I'm a new leader, what steps can I take to build momentum quickly and ensure a smooth transition to my new job?

- How can I best get the information I need to make smart decisions as a leader?

- What communication skills do I need to strengthen in order to get the information I need, define an inspiring vision, and win my people's commitment and best effort?

What Leaders Do—and Don't Do

. . .

Definitions about what makes a leader effective are changing. In this section, you'll find descriptions of the characteristics and abilities that today's business leaders must possess in order to generate results for their organizations. The picture isn't simple: leaders need to be both high-energy and energizing to those around them, and must demonstrate consistent values. They have to cultivate a shared sense of destiny among their followers as well as establish systems for allocating resources and measuring their teams' performance. And they must motivate their people to adapt to shifting business realities that require new behaviors, attitudes, and skills. No easy task—but the articles in this section can help you clarify the challenges facing you in your role as leader.

What You Can Learn from Jack Welch

• • •

Walter Kiechel

An icon is variously defined as a fixture in the popular imagination or the representation of a venerated personage. By either definition, Jack Welch qualifies as an icon. He's a saint, or at least a guru, to those who worship in the temple of results-oriented capitalism. To those nostalgic for the days when the workplace seemed more imbued with notions of community, he looms as the bogeyman, a symbol of the excesses of sharp-elbowed neo–social Darwinism.

Whatever your perspective, Welch, the head of General Electric for 20 years until his retirement in 2001, ranks as the most influential CEO of the last quarter century. (For our purposes here we'll consign Bill Gates to the "entrepreneur" category.) His achievements have done more than any other executive's to define the boundaries of what's possible, admirable, and acceptable in corporate practice today. In terms of rewriting whatever social contract existed between employer and employee in the U.S., GE led the way. Under Welch, the company blew out everyone's estimate of just how fast a venerable industrial elephant could dance, and across how wide a global stage. Any contemporary conversation about leadership in a business setting has to take Welch into account.

It will be at least another 20 years before we'll be able to see the full effects of all that Jack hath wrought—on GE, market capitalism, and the American social fabric. But the publication of his autobiography, unsurprisingly titled *Jack*, provides an occasion to revisit the lessons that managers may want to carry away from his example. This is a vein that book authors have been mining for a decade. What the autobiography adds, perhaps in part because it was written with distinguished management journalist John Byrne of *Business Week*, is context—the narrative arc of the man's life, a few windows on his psychology, even a little apologia here and there, this from an utterly unapologetic guy—context that illuminates particular lessons. In short, it's as close as we're likely to get to an instructive summing up from a man not at all inclined to be reflective. It's no accident that the book is subtitled *Straight from the Gut*.

Lesson no. 1:
Put the right people in the right jobs.

"Build" them—Welch's verb—with abundant and varied experiences. Conspicuously reward the best with opportunities, money, and praise. Never let them rest on their laurels—cull their ranks continuously. Welch doesn't set much store by corporate strategy as it was understood before his arrival on the scene. Indeed, one of his first acts as CEO was to abolish GE's planning apparatus, at that time perhaps the largest in the world. What he does believe in is the power of people, especially people who act a lot like him.

> Former GE vice-chairman Larry Bossidy once likened Welch's staff meetings to Miller Lite commercials— "loud, raucous, and animated."

At the top of his particular corporate heap are the A's, the best-performing 20% of the managerial cadre, who display the four E's of GE leadership: "very high *energy* levels, the ability to *energize* others around common goals, the *edge* to make tough yes-and-no decisions, and finally, the ability to consistently *execute* and deliver on their promises." Every year a business unit's leaders identify the A's, the B's who make up the middle 70%, and the bottom 10%. "The underperformers generally had to go," Welch notes, which is not cruel or brutal. Brutal is "keeping people around who aren't going to grow and prosper."

Apparently, no rising manager is immune from the process, or from the performance ethic that underlies it. Welch tells of hunting down Jeff Immelt, the man he would eventually pick to be his successor, at a management retreat in 1995. The plastics business Immelt headed for GE had missed its net income number by $50 million, and he was avoiding the CEO. "Jeff, I'm your biggest fan, but you just had the worst year in the company," Welch told him. "I love you, and I know you can do better. But I'm going to take you out if you can't get it fixed."

If this seems like overly tough stuff, particularly coming from a guy who worked at the same company for 41 years and who hates the nickname Neutron Jack, think of it as analogous to running a professional baseball team. You look for potential stars, bring them up through your farm system, pay them more than they can get elsewhere, expect them to hit .350 or to pitch 20 winning games a season, and let them go when they don't. Thus is a winning franchise built—and it's pretty clear that Welch cares more about winning than anything else.

Lesson no. 2:
Come up with a few key ideas.
Push push push them through the
company until they become realities.

In his 1998 book, *Jack Welch and the GE Way*, Robert Slater ticks off the major themes that the chairman has "campaigned" on, more in the military sense than in the political. In the early years, there was "be No. 1 or No. 2" in your industry; "fix, sell, or close" businesses that didn't achieve such dominance; and do it all with "speed, simplicity, and self-confidence." The initiatives from the late 1980s on, picking up the language from Welch's own book:

- WORK-OUT: a program of town meeting–like sessions to take "unnecessary work out of the system."

- BOUNDARYLESSNESS: the attempt to "remove all the barriers among the functions" in the company, "knock down external walls, making suppliers and customers part of a single process," put "the team ahead of the individual ego," and open GE up "to the best ideas and practices from other companies."

25

- GLOBALIZATION: the company's revenues from outside the U.S. surged from less than 20% of the total in 1987 to 40% last year.

- GROWING SERVICES: Welch thinks of this as mostly building on the company's medical-systems, power-systems, and aircraft-engines businesses, but an outsider might include the incredible rise of GE Capital, which in 2000 accounted for 41% of the company's total income.

- SIX SIGMA: the radical reduction of defects not only in manufacturing but in service processes as well.

- And inevitably in the latter part of the 1990s, E-BUSINESS.

Where other companies might loudly proclaim such initiatives but not actually do much with them, Welch put teeth into the effort, often by linking executives' advancement with the degree to which they rallied to the cause. Thus, by the end of 1998, "no one would be considered for a management job without at least Green Belt training"—the next-to-highest level—in Six Sigma. Infusing each campaign, too, is a sense that this is personal to Jack, maybe even tied into a particular stage of what psychologists might call his adult development.

Take self-confidence, which together with speed and simplicity made up a Welchian rallying cry for GE in the

1980s. Judging from his general boldness, you might think this has never been an issue for Welch, but you would be wrong, slightly. He titles the first chapter of his autobiography "Building Self-Confidence" and there credits his mother, clearly the dominant personage in his life, for instilling in him so much of the quality that he didn't worry about the stammer he grew up with and didn't even realize until years later how much smaller he

> Welch's antipathy toward bureaucracy seems visceral, animated, as toward a large, looming presence thwarting his efforts.

was than the others on the sports teams of his youth. Other fondly remembered mentors helped him see how important it was for a boss to build confidence in the people he's developing, particularly the confidence to share ideas openly. Self-confidence, he has observed, comes from winning.

The alternative to self-confidence is almost unthinkable. In one of the scarier passages of *Jack*, Welch describes the "GE Vortex," which occurs "when leaders lose their confidence, begin to panic, and spiral downward into a hole of self-doubt. I've seen it happen to strong, bright, and self-confident general managers of billion-dollar businesses. They were doing just fine in good times but then missed an operating plan or made a bad deal—not for the first time—and self-doubt began to creep in. . . . It's a terrible thing to see. Few ever recover." Jack's advice: don't go there.

Lesson no. 3:
Hate bureaucracy.

In its place, substitute processes and systems—regular meetings, appraisals, follow-up mechanisms—that allow people directly engaged in the work to hash things out informally, preferably face-to-face. Redo staff functions to support line businesses. Welch's antipathy toward the bureaucracy he experienced at GE before becoming CEO seems visceral, animated, as toward a large, looming presence thwarting his efforts. In 1980, GE had 130 vice presidents, 25,000 managers, and as many as a dozen levels of hierarchy between the CEO and the shop floor. Twenty years later, in a company six times as large, there are only 25% more vice presidents, fewer managers, and typically only six layers in the organization.

It comes as a bit of a surprise then to read of the relish with which Welch pursued a stupefying round of annual meetings. The January meeting in Boca Raton for the company's 500 top operating leaders; quarterly meetings

Welch
A Reader's Guide

You can fill a small bookshelf with works on the man and his practice, and you may want to. Besides *Jack: Straight from the Gut*, the ur-text for interpretation is probably *Control Your Destiny or Someone Else Will* by Noel Tichy and Stratford Sherman, with a chapter by the man himself. Robert Slater has published three books distilling Welch wisdom, including *Jack Welch and the GE Way* and *The GE Way Fieldbook*, almost a "For Dummies" guide in its here's-how applicability. Janet Lowe's *Jack Welch Speaks* offers a surprisingly good compendium of things Himself has said over the years, plus interesting quotes about him, some critical. For a full-bore critique, thorough in its journalism, consult *At Any Cost*, subtitled *Jack Welch, General Electric, and the Pursuit of Profit* by longtime *Wall Street Journal* reporter Thomas F. O'Boyle.

of the Corporate Executive Council; so-called Session C meetings in April and May, at which every unit reviews its talent portfolio, plus follow-up sessions in July and the fall; business reviews in June and July; the October annual meeting of officers; monthly meetings of the GE Capital board—you get the idea. But there is apparently nothing bureaucratic about these sessions, nothing cold or formal, nothing that would get in the way of a no-holds-barred discussion. As Welch recounts enthusiastically, Larry Bossidy, his good friend and a former GE vice-chairman, later

likened their staff meetings to Miller Lite commercials—
"loud, raucous, and animated."

In the course of dismantling GE's bureaucracy, Welch
also transformed important staff functions to the benefit of the operating businesses, though he regrets how
long this took. Maybe the best example was the company's finance and audit operation. This 12,000-person
institution had the best training program in the company, he writes, but was set in its ways, such that it was
"controlling the hell out of the place but didn't want to
change either the company or itself." Welch put a new
man in charge, a GE executive but one from outside the
finance area, who cut the staff in half, consolidated pay-
roll systems, and changed the training program to emphasize leadership and management as much as finance.
The result: a staff that has moved "out of the green eye-
shade 'gotcha' role" to become partners of the business
units, perhaps most notably by turbocharging the trans-
fer of best business practices related to companywide initiatives such as Six Sigma.

Lesson no. 4:
Talk straight, speak your mind, even to a degree bordering on brutal candor. Expect others to do the same.

If, per Emerson, an institution is the lengthened shadow
of one man, then chalk up to Jack Welch the degree to

which GE people can face facts and hash them out them productively, well beyond the norms that prevail at other companies. As one employee observed to the *Wall Street Journal* in 1988, "You can't even say hello to Jack without it being confrontational. If you don't want to step up to Jack toe-to-toe, belly-to-belly and argue your point, he doesn't have any use for you."

One of the unresolved questions about the Welch era at GE is how much pushback the man really accepted, how many arguments he was willing to lose. In a slightly bizarre passage in *Jack*, Welch describes his occasional "deep dives" into a particular challenge the organization might be facing—for example, the competitive threat to CNBC's *Business Center* show posed by Lou Dobbs' return to rival CNN's *Moneyline*. Welch would plunge into the problem, offering up ideas and solutions, but his people "knew that I didn't hold any hard feelings if my ideas got tossed in the basket." The sentence is followed by a parenthetical "(*Editor's Note*: The hell you didn't!)."

Candor apparently doesn't mean that you have to talk about things that you don't want to, at least if you're Jack. Among the most frequent criticisms of his auto-biography is that he doesn't say much about the end of his first marriage (of 28 years) or the issues that might be raised by having a CEO paid more than a hundred times as much as the lowest-paid employee of the company.

Lesson no. 5:
Do deals, launch initiatives,
keep the army always moving forward.
Act act act and don't look back.

Talk about a bias toward action. Has any one person ever fostered as much change and growth in a large company with a rich history as Jack Welch did at GE? The list of acquisitions made on his watch is by itself fairly staggering—forget the divestments. The accomplishment is extraordinary, not to mention the energy behind it. And yet Welch has long said that he doesn't see much point in reflecting on the past, which made working up his autobiography a different kind of challenge.

Lesson no. 6:
Always make your numbers.

It's how you know you're winning. And it also represents a handy alternative to the examined life.

For Further Reading

Jack: Straight from the Gut by Jack Welch with John A. Byrne (2001, Warner Books)

Reprint U0112A

The Work of a Modern Leader

An Interview with Ron Heifetz

• • •

Ronald A. Heifetz, director of the Leadership Education Project at Harvard's Kennedy School of Government, is author of the acclaimed book *Leadership Without Easy Answers*. In it he identifies six key components of leadership: "getting on the balcony," identifying the adaptive challenge, regulating distress, maintaining disciplined attention, giving the work back to people, and protecting voices of leadership from below. Writer Loren Gary spoke with him recently in his office.

You describe leadership as mobilizing people to face adaptive challenges. What do you mean by that?

If the solution to a problem is going to require social learning—people having to learn new habits, change their values or priorities or ways of doing business—you know it's an adaptive problem.

An adaptive problem as opposed to a technical problem, which simply requires the application of a particular skill or know-how. Is it really that hard to discern the difference between the two?

It isn't that hard. Sometimes, you do it by trial and error: You throw all your technical fixes at it and the problem's still there. But frequently you can, from the beginning, step back and say, "Is this problem going to require people to change their habits or learn new ways?" Another tell-tale sign of an adaptive challenge is conflict that doesn't seem to go away easily—for example, a conflict in values, or a conflict over strategy.

So why do you say that proposing technical solutions for adaptive problems is the most common mistake leaders make?

People gain authority in organizations because they get rewarded over and over for being good problem-solvers, for taking responsibility. And, of course, that's a wonderful thing, to be a person who's good at taking responsibility. But adaptive work requires getting other people to take responsibility—pushing the work back into the organization, getting other people to do the work that only they can do. You may have a proposed solution, but it doesn't solve anything unless it lives in people's behavior. So, you've got to somehow get people to learn new ways if you're going to solve these adaptive problems. And that requires a different mode of operating than being a responsibility-taker. It means being a responsibility-developer or a responsibility-giver. That's not the skill set that gets rewarded as you rise up the authority chain.

The successful manager's strength can, in fact, become his Achilles' heel when it comes to adaptive work.

Exactly. Especially in times of distress, people look to authorities to behave in the old responsibility-taking way. There's a lot of reinforcement for being the heroic, decisive answer-giver, rather than the question-giver. Treating adaptive problems as if they were technical is the classic error leaders make. Still, sometimes the reverse also happens.

How so?

People these days think that teamwork is the solution to everything, that flatness is always better. Although that's often true for adaptive challenges, it's not necessarily true for technical problems. For problems that are basically within people's know-how, it's a lot more efficient to give somebody the power to run with the ball rather than have everybody with the right knowledge meet endlessly.

We don't know when to use teams and when not to use teams. We don't know when to let the authority structure do its job and when to balance an authoritative style with a more participative style.

That's fascinating. The pace of change—in markets, technology, and among competitors— spurs businesses to focus on learning. Yet the anxiety caused by this seemingly accelerating pace of change fosters a crisis mentality, in which the organization yearns for the authoritative answer-giving characteristic of technical problem-solving.

That's true. The pace of change is so swift these days that most organizations are in a chronic state of crisis. And that tends to generate crisis behavior: long hours, pushing other things aside, as well as the kind of dependency dynamic that is responsive to an authoritarian kind of leadership.

One of the key sources of adaptive capacity is what I call the "holding environment." How much trust do people have in the authority figures—informal, as well as formal authorities? Because if they don't have much trust, it's very hard for authorities to raise challenging questions—people will make end-runs around them, or they'll wait until they have gone. Or they'll sabotage them.

So, trust is really a quite critical source of one's informal authority, and that trust enables you to hold people, hold people's attention to the hard issues.

If you're a new manager, and don't have a history with the people you're supposed to lead, how do you earn their trust?

People generate trust when they are predictable along two dimensions: in regard to their competence, and in regard to their values. If you're very competent, but people can't predict where your values are going to lead you, you become scary—you become a kind of Dr. Frankenstein. On the other hand, you could have your heart in all the right places, but if you're incompetent, people will also not trust you. The example here would be the wonderful family doctor whom everybody loves, but who doesn't keep up with the latest research and treatment methods anymore.

Trust requires predictability along both dimensions. People look to authorities to be competent, particularly when it comes to being able to mobilize solutions to *technical* problems. So, the first way one can demonstrate one's trustworthiness is to distinguish adaptive from technical problems, and be effective at mobilizing technical work. That is, being effective at taking charge, energizing your organizational system, and making sure that procedures get done right—supervising those kinds of problems for which you have the expertise.

Once you've built up a track record of being good at solving technical problems, then you can begin to spend that capital by saying things like, "Okay, you've seen that I'm competent at these problems. Now please trust me when I say that now we're also facing some adaptive

> "Leadership conceived as the lone warrior is really heroic suicide."

challenges. And they have to be handled differently. They require me to raise the key questions, but I'm not sure what the answers are going to be. They require me to tell you that we're all at risk here. I can't necessarily protect you from this reduced revenue stream. I can't tell you that I can keep your current way of operating, because this adaptive challenge is going to require us to move through a period of disorientation, until we develop a new orientation. I can't keep the conflicts under wraps, because the conflicts are part of our adaptive work. We have different viewpoints that we need to organize and come to terms with, so that we can create some innovations."

People aren't going to believe you when you say, "Let's do this adaptive work," if they don't already believe that you can do the technical work.

Let's look more closely at some of the components of leadership. For instance, what you call "getting on the balcony." How do already over-scheduled managers make time for that?

It's hard for them to make the time to step back and get an overview of the larger context, and of the politics involved in the change process. To do that, I recommend two strategies that are not used frequently enough. The first is that people need partners who can help you see your blind spots. Leadership conceived as the lone warrior is really heroic suicide. People need other people who can yank them by the collar and say, "Look, Jack, look what you're doing here! You're using that skill in the wrong place. Let's figure out how we're going to go back into that meeting tomorrow and make a mid-course correction."

Second, in rapid-paced, crisis-driven organizational life, you need a sanctuary. Just as you wouldn't go out into a Boston winter without a warm coat, you oughtn't think that you can lead people without having some place where you can get away from all of the people talking at you, all of the voices, all the calls—some place where you can quiet yourself and hear yourself think.

It might be a church or temple or synagogue or mosque, or it might be a running path, or a friend's kitchen table where you can have coffee, or a tree that you can sit beneath. We need places where we can reflect on the dynamics that surround us, and our purpose for engaging those dynamics in the first place.

What are some of the finer points involved in regulating distress within an organization?

The person in authority often thinks his job is to restore equilibrium. He doesn't realize that adaptive work often requires holding people through a sustained period of disequilibrium, during which they finally learn a new set of ways to do adaptive work.

The key is to control the pressure cooker, pacing and sequencing the issues so that people are working productively under the pressures. It's not that you, in participative processes, just throw the ball at people and let them run with it. You've got to keep monitoring and managing how people are doing the adaptive work.

How do you distinguish between having turned the heat up too high and having employees that can't take the heat?

There are a number of ways to reduce the level of distress and bring it down within a tolerable range. Changing personnel, so that you're dealing with people who have more resilience, more adaptive capacity, is just one of the ways. But there are others.

For example, if you're the authority figure, you tend to diminish the level of distress by becoming more of a physical presence. If people see you, they feel calmed; and particularly if they see you poised rather than flapped, they will take that as a cue that the situation is containable. If you appear present but panicky, they'll take that as a cue that they've also got to panic.

Furthermore, you can organize and structure the situation, the problem-solving. You can also work to generate bonds of identification among the people who have to do this work by speaking to shared purposes, shared history, shared culture, and values. The Japanese do all sorts of teaming exercises such as calisthenics as a way of developing shared experiences. Some companies have their employees do Outward Bound programs together. All of that soaks up anxiety and raises the limit of tolerance, so that people can operate at a higher level of distress.

Another thing the leader has to look out for is work avoidance. In other words, instead of facing the adaptive challenge, people frequently generate distractions. Or they'll define the problem too narrowly, so that the conflicts are avoided or submerged. They'll opt for a technical fix. They'll try scapegoating, or externalizing the blame. And of course, authorities routinely collude in such work avoidance.

I'm shocked. How do they do that?

By doing many of the same things employees do. Focusing on a technical problem. Avoiding the real conflicts that are in the room. Giving the problem to a committee and then killing the committee. Silencing dissenting voices in the meeting. Taking all the work on their own shoulders. Being the heroic answer-giver.

Are there gender differences in the way that leaders approach adaptive work?

Discussing gender differences lies always in the realm of making generalizations. And with any generalization, there are people who fall outside the generalization. But in my experience, men and women do have different challenges. Women are more at home with the idea that the job is not to take all the responsibility, but to develop other people's capacity to take responsibility. They're also socialized into knowing that listening is as critical as speaking, even more important.

Men have disadvantages along just those same dimensions. Men tend to take too much responsibility instead of passing it back. They like seeing themselves as decisive problem-solvers rather than mobilizers of other people's problem-solving. On the other hand, men are more at home with conflict. It's easier for men to imagine conflict being a source of creativity, a source of learning. Women are more at home with leading without authority, or leading with just informal authority. And men are more at home being authority figures.

Men have more to learn about how informal authority is a far more critical source of power than formal authority—the capacity to gain people's trust and admiration and respect, which form informal authority. Women have to learn to be comfortable seeing themselves in a formal authority role, and in serving those basic social functions that all authorities, and all managers, have to serve: direction, protection, orientation, control of conflict, and the maintenance of norms.

One last question. Some people work to live, while others live to work. Doesn't your theory of leadership assume that most people fall in the latter category, when, in fact, they don't?

I don't like the dichotomy you've made between working to live and living to work. It doesn't capture reality. People are more complex than that. And second, it's not even healthy, because when you set up a dichotomy like that, you force people to choose one camp—and I don't think people ought to be in either camp.

Implicit in your dichotomy is the assumption that people are either workaholics or apathetic, and that only the workaholics are responsive to a leader's attempts at motivation. The implication is that people don't want to do adaptive work because they're not much invested in their work to begin with. But I don't think that's true.

I think the people who are actually deeply invested find it just as hard, if not harder, to change, because they're already invested in their own way of doing business. They get a lot of personal satisfaction and organizational reward for acting a certain way.

It's not because of apathy that people resist adaptive work, it's because they care about what they do.

For Further Reading

Leadership Without Easy Answers by Ronald A. Heifetz (1994, Belknap/Harvard)

"The Work of Leadership" by Ronald A. Heifetz and Donald L. Laurie (*Harvard Business Review*, January–February 1997)

Reprint U9704B

Why Authority Still Matters

• • •

Loren Gary

What's the key to successful leadership? Two books use Martin Luther King, Jr.'s "I Have a Dream" speech to illustrate the art.

In the third edition of their classic book, *The Leadership Challenge*, James M. Kouzes and Barry Z. Posner argue that the speech's real power derives from King's ability to enroll his listeners in a shared sense of destiny that included their own hopes and dreams. In Kouzes and Posner's depiction, today's successful leader is rather like a persistent suitor: an ardent listener who wins the hearts of followers with his sincerity, his passion, and his ability to give voice to a vision roomy enough for others to recognize themselves in it.

Kouzes and Posner believe that heightened uncertainty across the world today has led to a "more intense search for meaning"; it has also prompted people to look for more from their leaders. Consequently, *The Leadership Challenge* emphasizes the relational and personal aspects of leadership. It's filled with discussions about how to set direction by inspiring, engaging, and empowering.

Noticeably absent from their analysis, however, is any direct treatment of the role of authority. In an age that so values empowerment and consensus building, has authority lost its place?

Certainly not, argues J. Richard Hackman, professor of social and organizational psychology at Harvard University. His book, *Leading Teams*, also discusses how to create the conditions that enable teams to manage themselves in the process of achieving performance levels far beyond what might be possible from a loose collaboration of individuals. But in marked contrast to Kouzes and Posner, Hackman takes pride in the fact that his book mentions the word *empowerment* only once.

For Hackman, what was significant about King's speech was the fact that he didn't "hold a national referendum to determine the aspirations of African Americans for the next stage in the struggle for racial equality. Instead, he exercised his considerable moral authority" to craft "a statement of direction that still inspires."

Of course, it pays to "consult widely with team members and other constituents about alternative aspirations," Hackman acknowledges. "But at some point those who

> **Unless leaders are unapologetic about exercising their authority, effective team self-management cannot occur.**

have the legitimate authority for the enterprise must step up to their responsibility and clearly designate the mountain to be climbed." Unless leaders are "insistent and unapologetic about exercising their authority," effective team self-management cannot occur.

The difference between Hackman's take on team leadership and that of Kouzes and Posner is subtle but significant. For Kouzes and Posner, team leadership often seems tantamount to empathy and cheerleading strategically applied. For Hackman, it is a psychologically darker undertaking, "an inherently anxiety-rousing activity" that involves "continuously balancing between tapping into forces rooted deep in the human psyche and finding mechanisms for channeling and controlling that energy."

Because direction setting requires the exercise of authority, team members tend to view the leader either as "an omniscient figure on whom they can depend or as an overcontrolling person who must somehow be repelled, subverted, or replaced."

And precisely because of these dynamics, team leaders must seek a balance "between assigning a team authority for some parts of the work and withholding it for others," Hackman continues. They must exercise authority sufficient to establish a unifying purpose without being so overbearing as to "invite significant performance problems or substantial underutilization of the team's resources."

The ideal blend of authority and latitude is achieved by specifying end states—the desired outcomes—without specifying "the details of the means by which the team is to pursue those ends," writes Hackman. Teams are able to do the kind of mindful processing required by work for which there is a low tolerance for error—for example, surgery, operating a nuclear power plant, or running an aircraft flight deck. This mindful processing also increases the likelihood that a team will come up with a genuinely creative idea or solution, "one that could never have been programmed ahead of time and, indeed, that may not even have occurred to those who created the team and set its initial direction," writes Hackman.

Teams can still function at a high level, but their performance has more to do with "the quality of the strategy dictated by the leader, coupled with his or her skill in motivating members to do exactly what they are told, than with the capabilities or potential of the team itself." Moreover, specifying the means in such detail often comes at the price of wasted human resources: you eliminate "the possibility of on-the-spot team improvisations that sometimes spell the difference between disaster and triumph" and run "the risk that members will become more invested in asserting control over their activities than in accomplishing well the team's main purposes."

When the leader specifies neither the ends nor the means, anarchy reigns. Teamwork quickly devolves into aimlessness, and members' motivation dissipates. But on teams in which the leader dictates the means without providing any explanation of the overall ends, is where you typically see a team at its worst, Hackman writes. Team members perform work by rote, with no understanding of how what they do fits in with what others do or how it contributes to organizational goals. Such a team's "products or services do not satisfy those who receive them, team capabilities atrophy or erode over time, and individual members do not find in their team experiences either professional learning or personal growth."

For Further Reading

Leading Teams: Setting the Stage for Great Performances by J. Richard Hackman (2002, Harvard Business School Press)

The Leadership Challenge by James M. Kouzes and Barry Z. Posner (2002, Jossey-Bass)

Reprint U0210D

Lead *and* Manage Your Organization with the Balanced Scorecard

• • •

Robert S. Kaplan

The current fascination with leadership is nothing new. Works as diverse as the Bible and *The Prince*, by Machiavelli, offer insight on the role of leaders in society. Leading management scholars, including Abraham Zaleznik, Warren Bennis, John Kotter, and Ron Heifetz, have contrasted the quite different roles and styles of leaders and managers. Leaders, for example, help people contemplate and adopt new ideas and approaches, while managers maintain stability and order. Leaders inspire employees to make day-to-day decisions that enhance an organization's long-term viability, while managers institute systems to ensure that all employees comply with top-down policies and directives. (See figure 1.)

Organizations, however, require more than just great leaders. They need executives who can simultaneously lead *and* manage. Executives must lead by continually adapting to dynamic, highly competitive environments;

FIGURE 1

Leaders Versus Managers

Leaders	Managers
Foster new approaches and ideas; alter organizational structures; cope with change	Conserve and maintain stability and order; cope with complexity
Shape moods and ideas; establish direction	React to goals
Welcome new options, develop choices, and stimulate fresh approaches to long-standing problems; choose which decisions get made and how vision and strategy get communicated	Keep choices and options down to manageable levels; focus on how decisions get made and communicated
Influence others to voluntarily make day-to-day decisions that enhance the long-term viability of the organization; maintain control through socialization, shared beliefs, norms, values; generate intrinsic motivation	Conduct day-to-day activities; negotiate, bargain, rely on extrinsic motivation; organize responsibility by functional areas of responsibility; conserve assets
Conduct turbulent, intense, and disorganized interactions that are future-oriented and involve risk-taking and creativity	Interact with people through prescribed roles and hierarchy

by communicating vision and strategy to employees; and by inspiring employees to innovate in order to achieve organizational objectives. But, at the same time, executives must manage by orchestrating a complex system of interactions that deliver organizational synergies, allocate resources effectively, align reward and incentive systems, and ensure that valid reporting and control systems are in place.

Historically, measurement systems have been used primarily to manage—for example, through budgeting, reporting, target setting, evaluation, and compensation. Many people may therefore be surprised to learn that a measurement system like the Balanced Scorecard (BSC) has been used by many executives as a powerful leadership tool. By studying their experiences, we learned how executives can use the BSC as a formal, systematic approach to simultaneously lead and manage their organizations to breakthrough success.

Duke Children's Hospital provides a good example of how an executive used the BSC to balance the dual roles of leadership and management.[1] CEO Jon Meliones had to cope with the open warfare between administrators and caregivers (the physicians and nurses). The administrators kept insisting, "Cut costs, save money." Caregivers retorted, "We're not good at cutting costs; we cure children and save lives. That is our mission." Meliones used the process of building a BSC to persuade everyone that they needed to do both to succeed. Certainly they had to lower costs (a management responsibility), but they also had to save lives (a leadership responsibility). He kept repeating to skeptics the Balanced mantra: "No margin, no mission," emphasizing the proper integration of management and leadership.

The Strategy-Focused Organization (SFO) framework (see figure 2) describes the five principles that organizations use to achieve breakthrough performance. The

FIGURE 2

The Principles of the Strategy-Focused Organization

principles transform the Balanced Scorecard from a measurement to a leadership and management system. Each SFO principle actively supports—indeed cultivates—leadership and managerial behavior.

1: Building the
Strategy Map and Scorecard

Leadership and management activities are central to the initial construction of a strategy map and Balanced Scorecard. Executives use the BSC first and foremost to articulate and communicate the organization's strategy—a leadership action, typically triggered by a changing, challenging environment. The process of building a BSC and a strategy map to describe the strategy helps an executive team develop fresh approaches to long-standing problems and create entirely new ideas for coping with change and challenges. The process shapes attitudes and ideas and establishes new directions for the organization.

The interplay of leadership and management duties occurs right at the top of any strategy map and BSC. The high-level financial perspective consists of two over-arching strategic themes: Revenue Growth and Productivity. The Revenue Growth theme requires leadership to identify new products and services, new markets, and the enhanced value proposition that broadens and deepens customer relationships. The Productivity theme, in contrast, calls for management practices that improve the utilization and efficiency of existing resources and processes.

2: Cascading the BSC Throughout the Organization

The second SFO principle, which involves cascading the strategy to decentralized divisions, business units, and support functions, is ostensibly a management function. It's the nitty-gritty of translating a high-level strategy into aligned and integrated substrategies throughout lower-level organizational units.

But the cascading and alignment processes themselves actually promote leadership at much deeper levels of the organization. Rather than senior executives dictating the company-level measures to the operating units, the cascading process encourages each operating unit to define its own strategy—based on local market conditions, competition, operating technologies, and resources—to deliver on the high-level strategic objectives. The most remarkable transformation occurs in support functions and shared-services units (like HR, IT, and purchasing). The cascading process transforms support departments from functionally oriented cost centers into strategic partners of line operating units and the company. As support departments gain the ability to articulate—often for the first time—their own strategies for adding value, their department heads become leaders. Before, they managed according to a budget. Now, they lead by developing a mission and a strategy for their respective departments.

3: Communicating, Aligning, and Rewarding

The third SFO principle involves three processes:

- Communicating the strategy (*lead*)

- Aligning personal objectives (*manage*)

- Linking variable pay to scorecard performance (*manage*)

Communication is clearly a leadership function. Effective, visionary communication is one of the most critical tasks of any organizational leader. The most successful BSC executives clearly understood the importance of communicating their companies' mission and strategy when they adopted the BSC. They saw the BSC as a highly effective way to deliver their message clearly and meaningfully to everyone in their organization.

Executives use the strategy map and scorecard to communicate the high-level vision, mission, and strategy to the entire organization. The communication process helps organizational leaders motivate their people and align them to the strategy. With a clear understanding of vision and strategy, every employee learns what his or her organization is trying to accomplish and how he or she can contribute to its goals. Such understanding generates intrinsic motivation. Employees come to work energized with the creativity and initiative to find new and better ways through which they can help the organization succeed.

The second and third processes—setting personal objectives and goals and rewarding individuals for accomplishing both personal and organizational objectives—fall within the management domain of an executive's responsibilities. Note how natural the flow is from the leadership functions (communicating, inspiring, and creating awareness) to the management functions (setting personal objectives and instituting incentive pay). By following the SFO framework, executives seamlessly integrate their leadership and management roles, contributing to the alignment of every individual with organizational objectives.

4: Integrating Strategy with Reporting Systems, Processes, and Learning and Growth

The fourth SFO principle also entails multiple processes:

- Integrating strategy with planning and budgeting (*manage*)

- Introducing new reporting systems (*manage*)

- Conducting the new management meeting (*lead*)

In a newly integrated planning and budgeting process, the executive team—through shareholder feedback and customer and competitor analysis—sets stretch-performance targets for the scorecard's strategic measures. These measures provide the basis for identifying and screening strategic initiatives that will guide the organization in achieving stretch-target performance. The integration with budgeting occurs when the team authorizes scarce resources (people, capacity, and funds) for the strategic initiatives. Finally, the organization links its strategy to existing organizational improvement initiatives, such as activity-based management and total quality management (including Six Sigma programs). All these practices—setting targets, screening initiatives, linking strategy to operational improvement programs—help executives deliver on their managerial responsibilities for strategy implementation.

The second process—introducing new systems for data collection and data reporting—is another central part of managing the business. Developing databases and new information systems may be laborious operational tasks, but they are essential for implementing new strategies.

The new type of management meeting, however, calls

for leadership behavior. Some aspects of periodic management meetings are routine—reviewing performance against plan (though now performance is measured by the scorecard measures, not just financial ones). But devising solutions to shortfalls, questioning the strategy, and searching for novel, interdepartmental solutions to fundamental problems requires leadership. Most important, leadership requires adapting the organization's strategy to changing circumstances. A good example of the contrasting purposes of monthly meetings is shown by the City of Charlotte, N.C. As a deputy city manager observed:

> (*Manager approach*) The previous city manager would review progress on a major project, like the Convention Center, to see whether it was on time and on budget. He would examine the causes of and cures for overruns and delays.

> (*Leader approach*) The new city manager is more strategic. She asks: "Why did we build the Convention Center? What is its impact on neighborhoods, on economic development, on employment, on downtown transportation, on the viability of downtown neighborhoods?" This is a much broader discussion, requiring the active involvement of people from many departments. The questions are bigger and harder but they are also more fun and more motivating.

(A leader questions the strategic implications of a project, not just whether it is meeting its milestones and budget.)

The most effective management meetings use double-loop learning, advocated by Chris Argyris, in which executives challenge the assumptions underlying their beliefs and strategy.[2] Executives test the hypotheses of their strategy, adapt their behavior based on what they have learned from recent operating performance, and examine whether external events may have invalidated their original strategic assumptions. During these meetings, executives also debate strategies that have been generated from within the organization. Henry Mintzberg and Gary Hamel have shown that effective leaders encourage new strategic ideas to emerge from anywhere within the organization, not just from the top.[3]

5: Mobilizing Change Through Executive Leadership

The fifth SFO principle—executive leadership—is not really a separate process. It pervades all aspects of the journey to breakthrough performance. Along this road, the executive leader plays three different roles:

- MOBILIZATION. Initially, the executive communicates the need for change and creates a coalition at the top to develop and deploy the strategy via strategy maps and Balanced Scorecards.

- GOVERNANCE. The executive establishes new systems for planning, budgeting, resource allocation, and reporting, and initiates the new management meeting. These actions reinforce the strategic message, keep the organization focused, and ensure that adequate resources are in place to accomplish strategic objectives.

- STRATEGIC MANAGEMENT. The executive reinforces the strategic message at every opportunity. He or she communicates with employees and questions managers about their contribution to organizational strategic objectives. He or she conducts the new management meeting, featuring double-loop learning, and asks "why, what-if, suppose that . . ." types of questions to emphasize learning and team problem solving.

All aspects of leadership and management become integrated as organizations apply the five principles to become strategy-focused. And rather than switch between leading and managing, executives embody both roles simultaneously and seamlessly.

The principles of the Strategy-Focused Organization and the BSC give executives a new tool for managing by customizing their organization's measurement and management systems for strategy formulation and implementation. But they also instill leadership as well as management behaviors and skills throughout the organization as the scorecard is cascaded out to local units and strategy becomes embedded in every improvement program and in the job of every employee. Among measurement and management tools, the unique property of the BSC to simultaneously promote leadership and management behavior provides organizations with a powerful advantage.

Notes

1. J. Meliones, "Saving Lives, Saving Money," *Harvard Business Review* (November–December 2000).

2. Chris Argyris, "Double-Loop Learning in Organizations," *Harvard Business Review* (September–October 1977).

3. H. Mintzberg, "Crafting Strategy," *Harvard Business Review* (July–August 1987); G. Hamel, *Leading the Revolution* (Boston, Harvard Business School Press: 2000).

Reprint B0207A

The Leader as Charismatic Hero: A Vanishing Breed

. . .

Too many leaders assume—wrongly—that a charismatic personality and take-charge attitude are all they need to enable their people to excel. It's hard to resist the temptation to rely on charisma alone to lead. After all, during times of rapid change or economic hardship, people *want* heroes who will give them all the answers and solve all their problems. But as the articles in this section reveal, providing answers and solving problems isn't leading. Instead, true leaders help their people learn to address their own problems with creative solutions and to develop their own answers. They make themselves available and offer guidance, all with an eye toward enabling followers to develop their own abilities. Real leaders may not make headlines—they tend to be modest, pragmatic, and more like plow horses than show horses. But they get the best results from their people.

No Time
for Happy Talk

• • •

Walter Kiechel

What do people want from the leaders of organizations? The answer that emerged with flame-bright clarity from the 2002 Burning Questions conference: more, more, more. Employees are anxious, clamoring for both reassurance and direction. Customers seem wary, desirous of a new deal. Investors, disillusioned big time of late, demand better stock prices now. Now more than ever, "the burden of leadership is extraordinarily high," says Ginger Graham, group chairman of Guidant, "and the work isn't nearly as pretty as it looks from the outside. So in a very real way, you've got to want it."

So much so that you're willing to put up with mounting levels of wear, tear, and the emotional drain that accompanies them. On the business front, consider this observation from Bain & Co.'s Chris Zook: 2001 was the highest year for CEO turnover on record. Some 22% of CEOs in major companies lost their jobs. The average CEO's tenure has now declined to only four or five years. Moreover, Zook's partner, Darrell Rigby, pointed out that although the recent recession, viewed in terms of GDP decline, has been mild, for corporate profits it has been the worst in 50 years.

Events beyond company walls have only added to the dismay: aftershocks from the bursting of the dot-com bubble; the collapse of the house of Enron and the ensuing allegations against Andersen; the unraveling of the telecoms; scandal in the Roman Catholic church; and, of course, September 11 and its aftereffects. Little wonder, then, that panelists at the 2002 Burning Questions spoke of "a more anxious environment." A "new fragility." And a dawning realization that our institutions, in the words of Daniel Goleman, coauthor of *Primal Leadership*, "have a life span, a natural history: they have an entrepreneurial beginning, followed by a mature phase, and then they pass on—they merge with another company, they're taken over, or they otherwise morph."

Obviously, the times are pushing organizations and individuals alike to ask, "What's essential?" Answers to this question, if you can pull back far enough to see them, seem to converge around innovation, broadly construed—

in how individuals lead, how firms exploit technology and relate to their customers, and how they define strategy and the core of what they do. A few insights—bubbles rising through the intellectual champagne of the conference's conversations—deserve special mention:

- "If you don't like bad news, you should get out of the leadership business," observed Kim Campbell, Canada's first female prime minister. It's not that you have to actively enjoy ill tidings, but "your job is to hear as much bad news as there is out there and to figure out ways of dealing with it."

- In considering where to put your information-technology resources, ask, "What's the locus of value creation in the firm?" Typically, it will be at the interface with the customer. Right now 70% to 80% of the IT budget in most firms goes to maintenance of the existing systems, but in five years all the infrastructure will be about driving innovation to the periphery of the organization.

- If the last 10 years have been about squeezing waste out of the company, the opportunity now lies in squeezing it from between a company and its suppliers and partners. One way to do this, in a Web-enabled world: figure out what you do best—and then outsource everything else.

- "Consumer" is a terrible construct because it leads us to think of the people who buy things as something less than complicated human beings. "Customer," by comparison, is more holistic; it acknowledges that individuals also have hopes, insights, and feelings—in short, that they are more than purely economic creatures.

Conference participants already understood the need to act upon these insights. So what was holding them back? More limited resources than in the ebullient late '90s, to be sure, and more anxious employees. But also, it seemed, an increasing disconnect between ideas, however exciting, and what their organizations were prepared to hear. For example, take these two notions about leadership that were presented at the conference: The way that top management teams manage their own emotions determines whether they will be able to take in new information or merely fall back on old routines. And many of women's leadership strengths, increasingly critical to organizations, derive from having been disempowered. In response to ideas like these, one veteran of the corporate change wars was heard to mutter, "How do I take that back to the guys at the company?"

The uncertainty about whether to push such ideas represents the flip side of the return to fundamentals that is under way in many organizations. Reacting to the excesses of the Internet era, managers are more circumscribed in their thinking, conference participants said, more focused on the bottom line, and so may be inclined to associate new ideas with additional costs.

Getting beyond that kind of thinking, and back onto the high road to innovation, will almost certainly require you to find modes of leadership appropriate to the situation. Understand that time frames are shorter: you'll need to get things done in six months or less, so you may want to emphasize smaller projects. Accountability—doing what you say you'll do—must be clearer, both your own and that of the people who work with you.

And as Harvard Business School professor Clayton Christensen's case study made clear, the principal enemy you'll encounter in doing the work of innovation will be all those corporate processes designed to ensure predictability and career safety.

What tools do you have at your disposal? Mostly your own integrity, the experts suggested—integrity understood in at least three ways. First, in the wake of Enron's collapse and the turmoil in the Catholic Church, it's important to realize that "integrity and transparency are of a piece," said Goleman. Not only must you be open to receiving bad news, you must also be able to perform what may be the more difficult task of giving bad news, as in quick and full disclosure. "It was easy when you were giving good news," said Ronald Heifetz, founding director of the Center for Public Leadership at Harvard's John F. Kennedy School of Government and coauthor of

Leadership on the Line. "That's what we've been doing for the last 10 years. But now you're distributing not pleasure, but displeasure."

You're presenting people with a "fairly conflicted set of questions," Heifetz continued. Your challenge is not to make the conflicts go away but to "orchestrate conflicts in a way that produces progress." In this realm, leadership is "as necessary on the periphery of the organization as in the center," and the greater the diversity—that is, the more varied the styles and perspectives—the better. Integrity here may consist of little more than simply staying in the game, week after week, in the face of all the resistance you'll get to the change you're trying to bring about.

Finally, understand that integrity probably means more openness about yourself—that transparency again—at times bordering on the uncomfortable. "You have to move from being a rational leader to being emotionally available," said Graham. "Employees want you to be available at a different level because they're searching right now. This makes for a leadership requirement that wasn't so present a few years ago." You're likely to find, as Graham did after September 11, that your people are asking with greater urgency than ever before, "How are you doing?"

And how *are* you doing? A less than honest answer won't do much to move the ball down the field in this tough game.

Reprint U0207E

Power

How Its Meaning in
Corporate Life Is Changing

• • •

Loren Gary

Right-thinking business people have probably always felt a certain ambivalence toward the concept of power: We acknowledge the existence of the thing, are often fascinated by its workings, but are usually a tad squeamish about applying the word to any aspect of our own situation. While we hurry to buy books that treat the subject indirectly—about which, more below—we tend to avert our eyes when someone wants to tackle the concept head-on. This is our loss, for a shared understanding of power and how it should work, even a subliminal understanding, informs how we manage and are managed. A look at the literature on power suggests grounds for hope that this common understanding has become more sophisticated over the last two decades, and that it may evolve even faster as we head into the 21st century.

Americans come at power with distinct cultural biases. In probably the most common view, power derives from a "mobilization of resources by one's own will," writes historian Gary Wills in his 1981 book *The Kennedy Imprisonment*, subtitled *A Meditation on Power*. As the founding of the Republic and the framing of the Constitution demonstrate, Americans have long been suspicious of institutional power. Over time, this mistrust has become translated into an attraction to charismatic power, defined by Wills as "a personal rule pitted against traditional and legal procedures."

In this mindset, the exemplars of powerful behavior are hero types who triumph not just over the enemy but also over the stuck-in-the-mud status quo at home, men like George Patton, Norman Schwartzkopf, or, in Wills's analysis, John F. Kennedy—PT 109 swashbuckler, Cold Warrior, bold proclaimer of the New Frontier, vigorous critic of the bureaucratic complacency of the Eisenhower administration. Applying the same kind of thinking to business, we make heroes out of Lee Iacocca, Ross Perot, and T. J. Rodgers—self-dramatizing figures who, while spending virtually all of their careers in organizations, rail against custom and procedure, cut through red tape, and make an end run around bureaucracy.

Underpinning our fascination with such figures is
what might be called the lowest-common-denominator
understanding of power, a view which, if seldom made
explicit, runs through many of those books on leadership and corporate strategy for sale at every airport book-
store. You know the genre: self-congratulatory, ghost-
written tracts by CEOs, football and basketball coaches,
politicians or political handlers, often produced at the
end of the author's career. Generally in such works,
power is a personal attribute, and of the most showy,
spectacular kind. Dig a bit deeper and you'll find that
frequently the power being discussed is, in essence, the
power to destroy. If that formulation sounds too strong,
just think of how many books you've read that offer tips
on how to "crush the competition."

Getting Beyond Power as Coercion

Fortunately, there has existed for some time a more
thoughtful literature on power and its applications in
corporate life. A seminal article, "Power Is the Great
Motivator," appeared in the *Harvard Business Review* in
1976 (it was reprinted in HBR in 1995), and sought to
overcome the squeamishness executives may feel about
wielding power. Based on extensive research, authors
David McClelland and David Burnham concluded that
the need for power is the most reliable predictor of managerial success, more reliable than the need for personal

achievement or the need to be liked. According to their definition, however, power is not the capacity to destroy, but rather, the ability to influence others.

The authors found the person motivated chiefly by a need for power to be the most successful at "creating an effective work climate." He tended to use his power for the benefit of the institution, rather than for his own benefit, leading McClelland and Burnham to christen him the "institutional manager." Institutional managers tended to join more organizations, and felt responsible for building up those institutions. They reported that they liked the discipline of work, and generally were more mature than those motivated by a desire for achievement or affiliation. Tellingly, and in contrast to much of the pop literature on power, the typical institutional manager also had a keen sense of justice, and a managerial style that was more democratic than authoritarian.

The 1985 book *Power and Influence* by John Kotter, formerly Matsushita Professor of Leadership at HBS, similarly demonstrated that, far from being uniformly corrosive—Lord Acton's "Power corrupts, and absolute power corrupts absolutely"—power is in fact necessary for the productive and creative resolution of conflicts within organizations. But Kotter's work also reflected a change under way across the corporate landscape. As he explained in an interview, "The management approach we've invented in this century achieves its influence through hierarchy. As interdependence increases through the growth in the number of people critical to the completion of a

task who are not part of the same hierarchy, the importance of hierarchy itself diminishes." These days, to
accomplish everything that needs to be done, managers
need access to kinds of power and influence that go far
beyond the capacity to hire, fire, and administer budgets.

Building on Kotter, Jeffrey Pfeffer's 1992 book, *Managing with Power*, provides an encyclopedic taxonomy of
these kinds of power and influence, as well as tactics for
using them in a complex organization. For example, he
describes the sources of power as structural, situational,
or personal. Personal sources, each to be drawn on as
appropriate, include focus, energy, stamina, sensibility,
flexibility, and the ability to submerge one's ego. He also
explains how the perception of power dynamics differs
according to one's location within an organization, and
how the use of interpersonal influence must be coordi-
nated with the management of information and analysis. Drilling down, Pfeffer delineates in detail how power
can derive from the control of resources, and from making those resources more important to the organization.

Of late, the literature on power seems to reflect a
pulling back from Pfeffer's kind of microanalysis to
focus instead on a more radical rethinking of the subject
and of the purposes to which power is applied. *Kinds of
Power* by depth psychologist James Hillman, published
in 1995, premises the importance of such rethinking on
the breathtaking assertion that it is not love, passion,
vision, nor even technology that are the truly formative
influences in our lives, but rather our perception of the

workings of business: "The drama of business, its struggles, challenges, victories, and defeats, forms the fundamental myth of our civilization." Precisely because of the centrality of perceptions of business to our everyday life, Hillman argues, the daily round of business is "where the contemporary unconscious resides and where psychological analysis is most needed."

Hillman's effort to "shower upon the mind of business the seeds of new thoughts for its activities" takes three approaches. The first is a cogently argued case—albeit a case that would strike the average business person as utterly seditious toward the current corporate establishment—for how a childish understanding of growth, an obsession with the principle of efficiency, an aversion to service, and the disparagement of maintenance have seriously degraded our social and natural environment. In contrast, Hillman holds up as an ideal the business that conceives of service as "a way of healing the world" and that operates by "raising the quality of whatever it touches."

The second approach consists of a careful turning over of words that have to do with power: control, office, ambition, reputation, authority, charisma, plus a dozen more. The result is a nuanced understanding of the ways power can be used, one far more supple than the monolithic conception of power as coercive force. For example, Hillman discusses "office" as meaning "duty to others," as "symbolized by the instruments of reception, from fax to waiting room. We perform service by taking in, hearing the others' requests." The final section of *Kinds of Power* looks at the mythological grids that form the substratum of much of our thinking about the future—for example, the myth of cyclical return, or of apocalyptic catastrophe. This section is a bit frustrating because it's not clear what we're supposed to do with the analysis. But that's precisely the point. The discussion of myths underscores Hillman's claim that power is not one thing, cannot be mastered by any single idea, or located solely in the agency of our will. The mythological grids point to agencies beyond human control; at least in some areas of life we are, to use Auden's phrase, "lived by powers we pretend to understand."

Hillman may sound radical, but one hears echoes of his thinking in what Harvard's Kotter says about the necessity to rethink the purposes of power. "Some of the most pathological organizations around have a lot of good parochial political players," he observes. "And they're getting killed in the marketplace. Increasingly, the challenge is not to make a few individuals more powerful, but rather to make the organization more powerful."

But how? "A lot of companies aren't thinking deeply enough about what their fundamental purpose is," Kotter explains. "But with the globalization of the economy and the incredibly intense pressure on businesses to perform, people are starting to ask how power can be used to help organizations meet their market and constituent demands. The focus for a company now is on the selection of the key tasks and core businesses. The companies that survive in the new economy will be those that, through a process of relentless self-examination, not only get their direction straight but also have their employees intellectually and emotionally convinced that their business creates something that adds value to the world"— this last note positively Hillmanian.

Transforming Yourself

Given such a climate, it's little wonder that so many companies have become interested in transformational leadership. Addressing this trend, *The Last Word on Power*, a 1996 book by consultant Tracy Goss, delineates the process of re-invention that a company's leaders must themselves undergo before any organizational transformation can take place.

Goss focuses primarily not on actions but on the quality of *being*—she almost always italicizes the word, which is probably a bit less daunting than using the Heideggerian *Dasein* throughout—from which thoughts and actions flow. She also pays careful attention to the importance of language in the construction of reality.

Part Zen teaching, part existentialist manifesto, *The Last Word on Power* tries to help you achieve some detachment from your most deeply embedded thoughts and feelings about yourself and the world. The liberation afforded by that critical distance enables you, according to Goss, to construct a future of your own choosing, and then make bold promises and adopt decisive action designed to make that future a reality.

For Goss, the power necessary for transformation is of a wholly different order than the kind of power that enables a company to, say, engage in a process of continuous improvement. It's the ability "to make something you believe could never come to pass, declare it possible, and then move that possibility into a tangible reality. Mastering this power gives you the capacity to act without being constrained by the habitual ways of thinking from the past—your own past, the history of your organization, and even the heritage of your culture. It allows you to act without feeling dependent on circumstances—without having to wait, in other words, for events to align in your favor."

Heady stuff—maybe too heady. Goss is right on the money when she argues that the uncritical application of strategies that have succeeded in the past can be a recipe for failure in the present. And what we call "reality" often turns out to be more malleable than we would have thought possible. But is it quite as plastic as Goss would have us believe?

Letting People Feel the Threat

Ronald Heifetz, author of *Leadership Without Easy Answers*, would almost certainly argue that it is not. His is a treatise in part on the constraints reality imposes on power.

Heifetz argues that leaders must engage in "adaptive work": testing reality, weighing the various interpretations of a problem and the evidence supporting them against other alternatives. Any vision the leader comes up with "must track the contours of reality; it has to have accuracy, and not simply imagination and appeal."

In the face of such pesky reality, perhaps the highest form of leaderly power is the ability to foster learning. With the most difficult problems, says Heifetz, "the problem definition is not clear-cut, and technical fixes are not available . . . Learning is required both to define the problems and implement solutions."

Leadership in such adaptive situations means "going against the grain. Rather than fulfilling the need for answers, one provides questions; rather than protecting people from outside threat, one lets people feel the threat in order to stimulate adaptation; instead of orienting people to their current roles, one disorients people so that new role relationships develop; rather than quelling conflict, one generates it; instead of maintaining norms, one challenges them." Not a bad prescription for the uses of power heading into the storm of change and opportunity that will be the 21st century.

For Further Reading

The Kennedy Imprisonment by Gary Wills (1981, Atlantic-Little Brown)

Kinds of Power by James Hillman (1995, Currency Books)

The Last Word on Power by Tracy Goss (1996, Currency/Doubleday)

Leadership Without Easy Answers by Ronald Heifetz (1994, Belknap Press)

Managing with Power: Politics and Influence in Organizations by Jeffrey Pfeffer (1992, Harvard Business School Press)

Power and Influence by John Kotter (1985, The Free Press)

"Power is the Great Motivator" by David McClelland and David Burnham (reprinted in the *Harvard Business Review*, January–February 1995)

Reprint U9610A

What Should a Leader Be?

• • •

John Hintze

Pity the modern CEO. There was a time when captains of industry steered their organizations for decades on end without having to fear for their jobs with every strategic misstep or slide in share price, as so many current leaders do.

On the other hand, pay wasn't quite as generous back in the day. Chief executives received handsome compensation, no doubt, but it looks modest when stacked up against today's multimillion-dollar salary-bonus-and-perks packages.

Leaders were once groomed quite differently as well.

Where top executives once came up through the firm's ranks, learning the business and the organization through years of direct experience, today CEOs just as often come from the outside. They are celebrity rainmakers brought in to shake things up and send that stock in the right direction. Or else.

Such is the state of leadership in much of U.S. industry: High-profile, short-term superexecutives who make a big impact on their organizations—at least at first—but who often don't have the chance to see the effect of their decisions over the long term.

If this is not the ideal scenario, then the question of the day becomes, What is? What qualities should we seek from leaders today? How long should leaders last? And how much of an impact do they really have anyway?

The CEO Effect

Between 1995 and 2001, CEO turnover at major firms rose 53%, according to a Booz Allen Hamilton study, while the average tenure of a chief executive dropped from 9.5 years to 7.3. And whereas the market once rewarded stability at the top, recent years have shown investors eager to wager on the arrival of outsider CEOs and their promise of new things to come.

Blame for this turn of corporate events has been heaped on several factors, such as the enormous influence of institutional investors on CEO tenure, and on the business press—always looking for the tales of glory their readers crave.

And with stories about a CEO's tragic fall even better, we have seen the rise of a culture of corporate stargazing, characterized by unrealistic expectations and swift punishment for failing to meet them.

"These expectations are formed in part by a fervent, though erroneous, belief that the quality of the CEO is the primary determinant of firm performance, and therefore that it's realistic to hope that a higher-powered CEO can be a corporate savior," says Rakesh Khurana, an assistant professor at Harvard Business School and author of *Searching for a Corporate Savior: The Irrational Quest for Charismatic CEOs*.

"There is no empirical basis in the hundreds of large-sample studies that there is a stable and direct CEO effect on firm performance," Khurana says. "This is not to say that CEOs don't matter. They probably do matter in very specific instances and certain kinds of contingencies, but this is not the theory that most people have in their head."

So was the popularity attached to charismatic CEOs over the last two decades by the press, business community, recruiters—everybody—as delusional as that attached to the technology bubble?

David Gergen, an adviser to four presidents and director of the Center for Public Leadership at Harvard's Kennedy School of Government, says there is a danger in *undervaluing* the quality of charisma in a leader, whether in business or in politics.

"People who have looked at it have said Cleopatra was not, by any means, the best-looking woman" of her time, he says. "But the fact was she had enormous presence.

> "A leader should be accountable for the value drives that create the context and the possibilities for the enterprise."

That's what changed history; it was her presence. And presence makes a difference in the quality of a lot of leadership positions. I don't think we should take it off the table as a quality."

However, he adds, "I think you can say it's been over-rated."

Scott A. Livengood, CEO of Krispy Kreme, offers another perspective, one that suggests that while the CEO's strategy—or vision—can have a significant impact on a company's performance, the personal traits of the individual executive are not necessarily so important.

"I believe a leader should be accountable for the value drivers that create the context and the possibilities for the enterprise," he says.

In 1996, Livengood notes, Krispy Kreme had a net profit of $1.9 million, an operating margin of 3.6%, and a private stock valuation of $35 million. "Last year, we earned a net profit of over $39 million. We had an operating margin of 14% and a market cap of around $2 billion. Now, I don't think I was as bad as the numbers would suggest I was in 1996, and probably not as good as our numbers were last year. But it was the same person, the same vision. It was just a different stage in the realization of the vision."

New Demands, Old Skills

No matter where you come down on the charisma debate, the hard business knocks of the last few years and the currently less than stable international and domestic environments have heaped new demands on corporate leaders. Now CEOs must deal routinely with developments that might spell disaster, whether they be SARS, war, or teetering into deflation. This new, unpredictable environment now necessitates broader, more practical skills as well.

"We're at a different point in time today," says Joie A. Gregor, president of executive recruiter Heidrick & Struggles. "It isn't about the charismatic leader as much as the whole leader, the broad-based executive. Today, you really have to demonstrate operating skills, and we look at that—it's a track record." For example, she says, "Is that CEO capable of putting in place—if it's not already there—the right team, and developing the right team?"

Gregor describes the current highest rung on the totem pole as someone with "basic leadership skills" enabling him or her to develop a corporate strategy with the help of the individuals within the executive team and the organization as a whole, and with the ability to articulate that strategy clearly.

Klaus Kleinfeld, the head of German conglomerate Siemens' U.S. operations—which employs 70,000 in the United States alone, more than Intel and Microsoft combined—puts forward a similarly pragmatic view of leadership. Kleinfeld, who held numerous and varied positions at the firm before becoming CEO in January 2002, says that while there are nuances in leadership style, the key ingredients of effective leadership are relatively consistent.

He lists eight principles that make up "excellent leaders," but only two involve individual character traits: Constantly raising the bar for oneself and being a self-starter. And Kleinfeld qualifies the second one, emphasizing the importance of communicating with more experienced superiors, to avoid making rash decisions.

The other characteristics he names range from being able to recognize that everybody contributes to the success of the organization, to leveraging team resources, to showing respect for employees, by carefully listening to them and making oneself easily accessible through the organization—not an easy task for Kleinfeld, with so many employees scattered throughout all 50 states.

Gergen notes that in the past we used to talk about the need for leaders to be persuasive, for the CEO to go out in front "for the corporation to talk to not only shareholders, but to employees and indeed to customers." Persuasiveness has often been associated with strong leadership, and the last two decades appear to validate that.

Kleinfeld acknowledges that persuasiveness is important. In fact, he calls it a "fundamental quality that goes without saying," much like the CEO making sure he or she remains physically fit. But somebody can have very strong communication skills, he notes, without being "what we used to call a charismatic communicator." What's important is to exhibit strengths in one-to-one or small group relationships, Kleinfeld says. "If that individual adapts [his] leadership style to his strengths, he can be an excellent leader."

But, Kleinfeld acknowledges, there does still seem to be a certain unknown leadership quality. He says a leader can make a "fundamental difference" by setting the tone from Day One. That's a big responsibility, and some charisma might help. But while a leader might set the tone, Kleinfeld suggests, he or she is not solely responsible for maintaining it.

The Intangibles and the Tangibles

The charismatic CEOs of the recent past were often brought onboard as corporate saviors, and they promised to bring intangible strengths like vision, values, and a sense of mission—a clear break from the company's past. But, HBS's Khurana says, the word *leadership* began entering the corporate lexicon only about 25 years ago, and the intangibles are more appropriately used in a religious context. In fact, he draws the parallel between the cult of personality endemic to charismatic CEOs and the real thing.

"The difference between a cult and a religion is that [the latter] outlasts personality," Khurana says. The danger with the charismatic leader is that the changes he makes serve more to glorify himself than to create long-term value for the company. Instead, we should seek leaders who "are oriented toward building long-lasting institutions," he says.

Terms like *values*, however, have been firmly established in the business vocabulary, and CEOs like Krispy Kreme's Livengood believe they are integral in promoting a company's strategy.

"I think words like that not only connect with employees, but they connect with customers," Livengood says.

He notes that Krispy Kreme was founded in 1937, but that its sales slowly slumped after its founder died in

1973, largely because its wholesale-oriented business strategy had become antiquated. By listening to customers, who wanted to see the doughnuts being made, the firm began pushing doughnut production out to its retail stores in the early 1990s, when he took over as president. It took time for the new strategy to work, but the company's net profits rose from $1.9 million in 1996 to $39 million last year.

Livengood, who has been with Krispy Kreme 26 years, since the age of 24, says leaders must be energized and engaged in the business. They must also be "obsessed with building a capable and cohesive team. They must think of themselves as teachers first and foremost, with the goal of making themselves less essential to the organization." And "they must view the success of the enterprise as a natural result of the growth and success of their people."

Khurana takes this a significant step further, saying that after a company's founder has set the firm's strategy, it becomes very hard to change in any significant way, so successive CEOs merely guide the ship and don't set the course. Indeed, to be a successful founder, one must create the conditions inside the firm needed to develop good leaders going forward. Situations may arise when a CEO dies or otherwise leaves prematurely before a subordinate has been groomed sufficiently, necessitating the recruitment of an outsider. But that outsider will have a managerial infrastructure already in place, and won't have to build one from the ground up.

Even with Krispy Kreme's significant change in strategy, Livengood notes that the firm's growth has resulted in large part from expanding and emphasizing existing parts of the business. And those decisions were clearly

> "I think leaders should last as long as they're energized about the business and its prospects."

made by leaders, like himself, who were groomed from within. Indeed, that concept appears to be paramount today, so that even recruiters like Heidrick & Struggles have come to terms with it.

"If you're in the search business and your approach is not to partner with the organization and encourage professional development, it's inappropriate," Gregor says.

About CEO Tenure

Perhaps a world of lesser expectations for the CEO will at least provide the benefit of extending his or her tenure at the company. But that still leaves the issue of when it is appropriate for a CEO to step down and let one of the groomed underlings take the helm.

There is a theory that a CEO performs best in the first half of his or her tenure. Most CEOs would probably disagree.

"I think leaders know when to leave when there are many people who could replace them," Khurana says. When a leader has developed the next generation to the point where he trusts them to take over, and thus he has made himself dispensable, "I think that's the real hallmark of a true leader."

Livengood adds, "I think leaders should last as long as they're energized about the business and about its prospects, and as long as they're meaningfully engaged in the business, that they're not withdrawing. They feel like they've done all they can do or it's time for somebody else to take over. And most importantly, they're creating long-term value for the company. To me that's the answer."

Reprint U0307A

The Call for Authentic Leadership with Bill George

· · ·

Bill George served as CEO of the medical technology company Medtronic from 1991 until 2001. Under his leadership, Medtronic's market capitalization increased from $1.1 billion to $60 billion, averaging 35% in growth annually, and earnings quadrupled. In his book, *Authentic Leadership: Rediscovering the Secrets to Creating Lasting Value*, George calls for current and aspiring leaders to take a good, hard look at their roles in business and in life.

When did you realize a moral compass would be essential to your role as a leader?

Early on I sensed business needed more ethically based leadership. I am appalled at the extent to which business leaders are caught up in the game of greed. We have idolized the wrong leaders, associating image with leadership and confusing stock price with corporate value. You cannot legislate integrity, stewardship, or good governance. We need a new generation of corporate leaders to restore the public trust in our corporations, what I am calling "authentic leaders."

What defines "authentic" leadership?

Authentic leaders have a deep sense of purpose for their leadership and are true to their core values. They are people of the highest integrity who are committed to building enduring organizations. Authentic leaders see themselves as stewards of the assets they inherit and servants of all their stakeholders. They lead with their hearts, not just their heads, yet they have the self-discipline to produce consistently strong results.

For example, there were occasions when we learned of problems with our products that were being reported, but where red tape was impeding the feedback getting to our engineers. As authentic leaders, it was our responsibility to fix these problems as soon as possible in order to be what we wanted to be as a company.

How do you transmit your ethics and values to others?

You must communicate the mission and the values of the organization every day, and the decisions you make must be consistent with these values. You can't do this sitting on a corporate jet. Employees watch your every action and want to understand the basis for management's decisions.

There is no substitute for personal interaction with employees and customers. Your employees learn from your behavior, how you treat people, and how you communicate with people.

When were your values put to the test at Medtronic?

Shortly after I joined Medtronic, I promoted a key executive to head our European operations. Four months later the head of our internal audit came to me with concerns about an unusual "promotional account" in this executive's former subsidiary. We appointed a special investigator to look into this account. His report indicated the likelihood that the funds were being used by our Italian distributor for payments to Italian physicians. So I called our executive and asked him to come to Minneapolis immediately to discuss the fund.

When I asked him about it, he said, "You don't want to know about that fund." When I told him that indeed I did, he accused me of imposing American values on Europeans. I told him directly: "These are not American values. They are Medtronic values that apply worldwide. You violated them, and you must resign immediately."

We decided to be completely open about what had happened and informed employees, the public, and appropriate governmental agencies. However, I blame myself then and now for not carefully checking out his values and business practices before appointing him.

How does one bring personal authenticity into one's business life?

This is the No. 1 question on the minds of young leaders today, as many feel squeezed between the requirements of their jobs and their desires to spend more time with their families, especially those with two-career marriages. Although the pressures of society and work often cause us to behave differently in our work and home lives, I believe we must resolve to knock down these artificial walls and behave the same at work and at home. It took me many years of effort to get there.

In the long run, leaders who find an appropriate balance between work and home life are more effective on the job. They make more thoughtful decisions and their employees make higher levels of commitment to the organization.

Reprint U0310D

In Praise of Pragmatic Leadership

• • •

Loren Gary

"Where there is no vision, the people perish," says the proverb. Especially in times of crisis, people turn to the charismatic leader because his vision offers clarity and instills confidence.

But charismatic leadership also has a downside. "It plays on people's weakness," says Rakesh Khurana, assistant professor of organizational behavior at Harvard Business School. "It offers people a way of escaping their responsibilities and the burden of having to make decisions."

Even though the limitations of charismatic leadership in a business context have been well documented over the past decade, the cult of the heroic leader remains strong. In the often dim light of an uncertain economic climate, this tendency to place too much hope in the ministrations of a golden-throated CEO threatens to undo many a company.

It's not that vision is unimportant, it's that something else is even more vital right now.

An ongoing study of 40 Fortune 500 firms conducted by the Center for Effective Organizations at the University of Southern California and the management consulting firm Booz Allen Hamilton concludes that "the CEOs whose companies are best weathering the recent downturn are practicing old-fashioned, pragmatic management by the numbers," write Bruce Pasternack and James O'Toole in a recent article in *Strategy + Business*. When the road ahead is unclear, vision can take you only so far.

How Things Got This Way

During the 1980s, "a long-standing decline in corporate profits ushered in today's era of investor capitalism," writes Khurana in a *Harvard Business Review* article. "Investors were suddenly looking for CEOs who could shake things up and put an end to business as usual." An "almost religious conception of business" emerged, "exemplified by the appearance of words such as 'mis-

> We've oversold not just the notion of charisma but the whole concept of leadership per se.

sion,' 'vision,' and 'values' in the corporate lexicon." The charismatic leader was "supposed to have the 'gift of tongues,' with which he could inspire employees to work harder and gain the confidence of investors, analysts, and the ever skeptical business press."

Although Khurana acknowledges that there are times when charismatic leadership is useful, "the widespread quasi-religious belief in the powers of charismatic leaders exaggerates the impact CEOs have on companies. We tend to think leaders have much more power and far fewer constraints than is really the case," he explains in a recent interview.

For example, in the airline industry, American's failure to successfully emulate Southwest's strategy should not be interpreted as a result of poor leadership. Rather, "the difficulty American is experiencing now is the result of decisions made years ago that constrain its current options."

"In the past two decades, we've oversold not just the notion of charisma but the whole concept of leadership per se," Khurana continues. "We've made this artificial distinction between leadership and management, failing to recognize the overlap—that is, the degree to which effective leadership requires managerial skills and vice versa."

Plow Horses, Not Show Horses

Management researcher and author Jim Collins characterizes this undervalued managerial perspective as the "ultimate pragmatism." Research for his acclaimed 2001 book, *Good to Great*, started with the question "How do you bring about fundamental change in sustainable ways?"

"We found only 11 companies that made the leap from mediocrity to truly superior performance that lasted at least 15 years," he says. (Collins looked for companies that had 15 years of cumulative stock returns at or below the general stock market, then a transition point that was followed by cumulative returns at least three times the market over the next 15 years.)

Does a charismatic style of leadership account for the transformation of these 11 companies? Collins's answer is a resounding "no." When looked at against the leaders of the comparison companies—firms such as Eckerd, A&P, and Scott Paper, which were in the same industries as the good-to-great companies but failed to make the leap from good to great, or firms such as Hasbro and Rubbermaid, which failed to sustain the shift from good to great—the leaders of all 11 good-to-great companies were "plow horses as opposed to show horses," says Collins, "dogged, determined, and disciplined. They didn't lead by having inspiring personalities as much as by having inspiring standards. They didn't create names, taglines, and events to trumpet things they wanted to accomplish. Instead of being high-profile change agents, they were a lot like tofu: clearly part of the meal, perhaps even the main source of nutrition, but the spice was provided by everyone around them.

"And although they've sometimes been portrayed as self-effacing, they were in fact very ambitious and also very willful. But their ambition was first and foremost for the cause, the company, the work. And they had the will to carry out that ambition."

Example: Darwin Smith, CEO at Kimberly-Clark. He had the courage to sell off the paper mills, the historic core of the company, because that was necessary if the company was to be not simply above average, but excellent. "The good-to-great leaders were the ultimate pragmatists in their focus on what was best for their company over the long term," says Collins. "They understood that you build greatness by laying a foundation, building it brick by brick."

Two key insights were central to their pragmatism:

- First, get the right people on the bus. With the right people in the right positions, you don't have to worry about motivating them—they'll be self-motivated.

- Acknowledge the facts. "One of the single most de-motivating actions you can take is to hold out false hopes," Collins writes in *Good to Great*. Yes, leadership is about vision, but it is "equally about creating a climate where the truth can be heard." The good-to-great companies had a vision for greatness, "but, unlike the comparison companies, [they] continually refined the path to greatness with the brutal facts of reality."

Execution: Bringing the Rhetoric Down to Earth

Instead of trying to revolutionize their industries, Larry Bossidy, the former chairman and CEO of Honeywell, believes that companies should focus on taking their businesses to the next level. "Unless you translate big thoughts into concrete steps for action, they're pointless," he writes in his new book, *Execution*. "Without execution, the breakthrough thinking breaks down, learning adds no value, people don't meet their stretch goals, and the revolution stops dead in its tracks."

But even people "who pinpoint execution as the cause of failure tend to think of it in terms of attention to detail," Bossidy continues. Execution is not to be confused with tactics—or micromanagement. It's just as

> # Execution is just as much an intellectual challenge as vision setting and strategic thinking.

much an intellectual challenge as vision setting and strategic thinking, but it has a decidedly granular cast.

Think of it as the formal and disciplined integration of three distinct processes:

- THE STRATEGY PROCESS: What's the plan for getting to the next level?

- THE PEOPLE PROCESS: Which people will do the jobs and how will they be held accountable?

- THE OPERATIONS PROCESS: What human, production, and financial resources will we need to execute the strategy?

As you study the intersections of these three processes, carefully examine all the alternatives that present themselves. Should you try to ride out the current period of slow growth? Invest aggressively? Radically downsize? Or rethink your core businesses?

In times of uncertainty, it's this commitment to an analytical process that companies need most, says Khurana, even though their tendency is to look to charismatic leaders to give them the answers.

Charismatic leadership's response to uncertainty is to offer followers an emotional rescue, explain Michael Mumford and Judy Van Doorn in an article in *The Leadership Quarterly*. Personal faith in the leader gives followers a sense of identity and purpose. Pragmatic leadership, however, takes a more functional approach to uncertainty. The focus is on problems and the rapid dissemination of new ideas and new forms of social organization that help eliminate those problems.

So which do we really need more of right now, faith or hard-nosed thinking? As Benjamin Franklin wrote in *Poor Richard's Almanac*, "In the affairs of this world men are saved not by faith but by want of it."

For Further Reading

Execution: The Discipline of Getting Things Done by Larry Bossidy and Ram Charan (2002, Crown Business)

Good to Great: Why Some Companies Make the Leap . . . and Others Don't by Jim Collins (2001, HarperBusiness)

"The Curse of the Superstar CEO" by Rakesh Khurana (*Harvard Business Review*, September 2002)

"The Leadership of Pragmatism: Reconsidering Franklin in the Age of Charisma" by Michael D. Mumford and Judy R. Van Doorn (*The Leadership Quarterly*, Autumn 2001)

"Yellow-Light Leadership: How the World's Best Companies Manage Uncertainty" by Bruce A. Pasternack and James O'Toole (*Strategy + Business*, Second Quarter 2002)

Reprint U0211C

10 Myths About Post-heroic Leadership—and Why They're Wrong

• • •

David Stauffer

"There is little doubt that if the humanistic or 'bottom-up' concept of leadership could be introduced and accepted on a company-wide basis and sponsored by the company's president," wrote consultant Robert N. McMurry in a *Harvard Business Review* article over 40 years ago, "it would make possible increased productivity, even under pressure, without adverse effect on morale. But since it cannot, benevolent autocracy is the most promising alternative." Successful companies, he continued, needed "aggressive (often hypomanic), hard-driving, and self-reliant" leaders at the top.

Increasingly over the past generation, however, companies have been trying to do precisely what McMurry deemed so quixotic: build genuine bottom-up organizations. *Managing for Excellence*—a 1984 book by David L. Bradford, senior lecturer at Stanford University's Graduate School of Business, and Allan R. Cohen, chief academic officer and professor of leadership at Babson College—became one of the foundation documents of this movement. Bradford and Cohen called for a "post-heroic" conception of workplace leadership, one based on "shared responsibility," to replace the "out-dated and inadequate" Lone-Ranger-rides-to-the-rescue model that had held sway for so long. Their follow-up book, *Power Up: Transforming Organizations Through Shared Leadership*, continues the discussion. It portrays the post-heroic manager as someone who sees everyone as a leader, who views her primary function as the building of a strong team with a common vision and mutual influence, who invites other employees to share the responsibilities of managing—thereby producing better decisions and ideas, more learning, and higher morale.

Sounds like a description of corporate Shangri-La: improved productivity and reduced managerial isolation and exposure, both as a result of sharing the burdens of leadership. Given the self-reinforcing nature of the most unsavory aspects of heroic management, who wouldn't be drawn to the post-heroic model? Well, apparently, quite a few executives—if the prevalence of the CEO-as-Patton genre of leadership tomes in airport bookstores is any indication. The reasons, upon reflection, should not surprise.

Leaders accomplishing Herculean tasks. Cutting through the Gordian knot of bureaucratic snarls. Bearing the weight of the corporate world on their shoulders. Effortlessly spinning out breakthrough strategies that are inspiring in their outline and full-blown in their attention to detail. The heroic model of leadership is brimming with a potency of mythological proportions. By contrast, the post-heroic paradigm seems, to many, to call for Casper Milquetoast with a counseling degree.

This is where the new paradigm gets distorted, counter Bradford and Cohen. What follows are "ten of the most frequent 'myths' (misunderstandings) about post-heroic leadership," along with corrective commentary provided by the authors in the revised edition of *Managing for Excellence,* in *Power Up*, and in interviews with *Harvard Management Update.*

Myth #1: It's most important to have people feel good, get on well, and have little conflict

Bradford and Cohen realize that "warm feelings may grow out of team and relational development." But those feelings are not the main goal: "Openness, vulnerability, and conflict are the continuing conditions of leading in the new way. . . . [Team members'] differing vantage points, expertise, and experiences will lead them to different views, which are key to excellent decisions."

The manager's key challenge here: dissuade team members from "a natural tendency to pull punches," especially on important issues.

Myth #2: Managing post-heroically is a "soft" way to manage

"Wrong," snaps Cohen. "It's a model for delivering performance, not for making nice. . . . To be post-heroic demands a toughness that few managers, even those who pride themselves on being hard, ever show. It requires the willingness to talk straight and encourage the same back from direct reports, even when dealing with delicate style or interpersonal problems." Examples of such toughness include not allowing team members to "delegate problems upward" (i.e., to you); tolerating, and even encouraging, confrontation, particularly when performance (including your own) is lagging; and being able to show personal vulnerability by openly admitting when you "don't know an answer or are in trouble."

Myth #3: The emphasis on collaboration means that members have to stifle their competitive urges

"Internal collaboration must be directed toward meeting external competition while internal competition remains an important energizing force," Bradford and Cohen acknowledge. "However, the internal competition must be against objective measures of success, such as past performance, benchmarked standards, and/or individual potential"—not against other colleagues. "Team members (and departments) will inevitably compare themselves to each other, but the comparison process must not deteriorate into doing each other in." The leader's challenge, therefore, is to steer the team away from both extremes—encouraging "personal striving," but not to the point that it "turns into interpersonal domination."

Myth #4: The post-heroic leader acts as a facilitator and is not allowed to be decisive

"Post-heroic leaders may be very decisive in dictating what the task is, without personally dictating or maneuvering toward the answer," write Bradford and Cohen. "This does not mean that the post-heroic leader can't express his or her opinions." In fact, "the leader can still make decisions. But where heroic leaders demand that the team settle on the leader's solutions to tasks, post-heroic leaders can demand that the team grapple with the unresolved, critical issue." The recommended approach would be, "Our job today is to determine how we are going to cut the budget," not, "Here are the cuts and where they must be made," or (by implication), "Keep guessing till you arrive at the cuts I want."

The post-heroic model does require leaders to think and act in very different ways, admits Tom Roth, vice president of international executive trainers Wilson Learning Corporation. "At first, they're thinking, 'You're asking me to give up a lot.' But later it's, 'You know what—this strengthens my role rather than weakening it.'"

Myth #5: If the leader makes autonomous decisions, then he or she is being heroic

Not so, say Bradford and Cohen: "There may be times when the leader finds it necessary to make a decision autonomously, or to override a team decision that has been made without sufficient information, or by a process that ignores critical considerations." But the conditions under which a team decision is overruled are necessarily limited and restrictive, because "leaders forgo exclusive veto power when they adopt shared responsibility." This loss is offset by the improved quality of the decision making. In the words of legendary baseball pitcher Satchel Paige, "No one of us ain't as smart as all of us."

When will the leader be most likely to act autonomously? According to Bradford and Cohen, "a topic may be so trivial that discussion of it would waste the group's time, or an emergency may demand immediate action, or the leader may have access to privileged information that can't be shared. Members will accept the leader's acting autonomously in these and similar situations, if they see that critical decisions are brought to the team."

Myth #6: Managing post-heroically means all decisions must be made by group consensus, and the leader has to accept these decisions

Bradford believes this myth arises from managers' desire "to see complicated new techniques simplified to specify what to do or not do under all circumstances." But effective leaders use at least four decision-making approaches, depending on circumstances: autonomous, delegating, consultative, and joint (i.e., by consensus). "Post-heroic leaders," Bradford continues, "reserve joint decisions for core strategic decisions, where everyone's contribution and full investment is needed."

The key, then, is understanding not only what shared responsibility is, but also what it is not. "Despite shared responsibility," write Bradford and Cohen, "the leader never escapes formal accountability for unit performance or for the decisions of the unit, by whatever method they are made. It is never acceptable for the leader to say to his or her boss, 'Sorry, I didn't want to make this decision but I had to go along with my team.'" Moreover, says Roth, "Leaders complain that once they share any responsibility with the team, the members will want to have a voice in everything. But in practice, what team members seem to want is not to run the show, but to be invited to have a hand in running the show."

Myth #7: Team commitment to a decision is more important than the quality of the decision itself

"[C]ommitment is important," the authors write, but focusing on commitment "can lead to compromises 'just to make everyone happy' or, worse, it can lead the manager into a compromising stance." In the post-heroic model, both the decision process and the quality of the decision itself are critical. Leaders should neither implement a sham version of shared responsibility—in which team input is sought but ignored—nor delegate responsibility so that they "don't have to do anything more."

For Roth, shared responsibility is neither delegation nor abdication—it's a mutual influence process. The goal, he says, is to reach the point at which both leader and team members recognize "we have a commonality of purpose and intent. They understand that we each have the other's best interests in mind, and we each have the ability to help the other grow and develop. Formal positions and titles and roles become irrelevant."

Mutuality doesn't develop overnight, Bradford and Cohen caution—especially when the leader is used to making all the important decisions "and subordinates are accustomed to delegating upward. But the resulting superior decisions lead to greater commitment to implementation."

Myth #8: Vision is the exclusive domain of the organization's leader

In some organizations, Bradford and Cohen observe, "creative entrepreneurial leaders have personally crafted compelling visions and then enrolled talented people to pursue them. . . . Solo vision formulation saves time and avoids the problems created by dissenting individuals. In most cases, however, involvement by the team leads to a richer, more potent vision, since members have differing perspectives about customer needs and ways to serve them. . . . Team involvement in formulation also prepares the way for participant commitment to embed vision in practice at every level."

Myth #9: Managing post-heroically tends to be slow and cumbersome

This myth arises largely from fear of meetings. While it's true that "meetings held by post-heroic leaders are less predictable and potentially more volatile," Bradford and Cohen maintain that post-heroic leaders will realize a net saving of time and energy when it comes to meetings about critical issues. "Traditional leaders," they point out, "are accustomed to meticulous meeting planning and spend a great deal of time thinking through everyone's likely responses, lobbying individual members before meetings, and planning how to get the right outcomes. In the post-heroic world, this is time wasted and a deterrent to superior collective decision making."

Myth #10: The benefits of post-heroic leadership cannot be seen in the short term

On the contrary, Bradford and Cohen write, for the post-heroically managed team, "dealing with core issues boosts performance immediately," and as the team coalesces, "productivity rises further." Which is not to suggest that the post-heroic model will yield good things more quickly than heavy-handed heroic measures, says

Cohen, citing the slash-and-burn management style of the self-proclaimed "mean" CEO Albert J. ("Chainsaw Al") Dunlap. "He's a turnaround manager who has consistently been able to show immediate great financial results with classically heroic action. But does his style build long-term value, bring successful new products to market, or develop employees?"

Although some improvements become manifest rather quickly, Bradford and Cohen still advise the post-heroic leader to "think in incremental terms, asking, 'How much can the team handle now . . . and what can be done to stretch them to take more responsibility in the future?' This does not mean 'development now for payoff later'; it is both at once." Good results can be slowed when a manager must go solo down the post-heroic path in an organization that's not going with her. "It is possible to create the post-heroic environment in your part of the organization," says Cohen. "But you have to recognize that this or any new and different practice is always harder if you aren't in a conducive environment. In those cases, you must have a greater measure of conviction. You must also be someone who's not afraid to break the organization's rules or violate the managerial culture for the ultimate good of the organization."

"Implementation of the post-heroic system is more complex than we had assumed," write Bradford and Cohen. The persistence of these ten myths reflects the difficulty of the shift in attitude and behavior that post-heroic management demands of leaders and followers alike. Then, too, each myth contains at least a partial truth—one that obtains most during the early stages of implementing post-heroic practices. For example, when leaders first attempt to run team meetings in a shared leadership mode, Bradford and Cohen write, "they find themselves in the middle of highly contentious meetings," feeling that they have lost all decision-making authority. "Their impulse is to grab back control."

Add to that the probability of greatest resistance at the top of the organization, where managers "have climbed the farthest and fastest under the now-outmoded model of leadership," Bradford observes. "These are the people who are most likely to have grown cautious about any new practice. To them, there's more downside than upside to any major change."

"When they've had time to grasp the implications, managers say, 'Wow, this isn't going to be easy,'" observes Roth, who developed and implemented post-heroic training based on *Managing for Excellence*. All reluctance aside, the smart money says that post-heroic management is what gets results in today's economy. Though often caricatured as touchy-feely and process-obsessed, post-heroic leadership, as Bradford and Cohen demonstrate, calls for decisiveness, sangfroid, and results-oriented thinking in no small measure. The transition requires "a leader with a solid sense of self-worth and self-confidence," concludes Roth, one who is comfortable creating the conditions that enable subordinates to excel, instead of providing all the answers.

For Further Reading

Managing for Excellence by David L. Bradford and Allan R. Cohen (1984, revised 1997, John Wiley & Sons)

Power Up: Transforming Organizations Through Shared Leadership by David L. Bradford and Allan R. Cohen (1998, John Wiley & Sons)

"The Case for Benevolent Autocracy" by Robert N. McMurry (*Harvard Business Review*, January–February 1958)

Reprint U9804A

Starting Out on the Right Foot

• • •

Are you assuming a leadership role for the first time? If so, you'll want to establish early successes that you can build on later in your tenure. After all, for most new leaders, their peformance during their first thirty days on the job can set the stage for success or failure later. The articles in this section help you start out on the right foot—by learning how to delegate; directing your own development as a leader; setting the right expectations for your boss, peers, and direct reports; and avoiding the problems that can arise when you replace a beloved predecessor. You can't anticipate every challenge you'll encounter as you ease into your new role. But with a little preparation and focus, you can plant the seeds for a successful tenure.

Debriefing Linda A. Hill

Accelerating the New Manager's Start

• • •

Lauren Keller Johnson

Making the leap from individual contributor to manager counts among the most challenging transitions in business life. New expectations, a new identity, new performance criteria—all of these can set a first-time manager's head spinning. Though newcomers to the managerial role must master the transition primarily through old-fashioned on-the-job experience, their bosses should help speed the process. Otherwise, seasoned executives may end up watching helplessly as their protégés make one too many irreparable missteps. In an age when a company's success hinges on its ability to attract top-notch talent and find people who can manage that talent, every executive must master the art of managerial development.

"Among all the challenges facing new managers, the need to reconcile different constituencies' expectations and interests is probably the most difficult," notes Linda A. Hill, the Wallace Brett Donham Professor of Business Administration and faculty chair of the Leadership Initiative at Harvard Business School. The expectations and interests of these constituencies—which include a manager's direct reports, her boss, her peers, and the company's customers—can conflict. For example, a manager's supervisor may want her to delegate certain tasks to her direct reports, but these same reports may expect lots of handholding. Balancing such competing demands is a must.

"If you're supervising a first-time manager," Hill says, "you'll likely see him worrying most about his direct reports' demands. Explain that he has to manage his other constituencies just as carefully."

Bosses must teach new managers how to exercise influence with constituencies over which they have no formal authority. "Many new managers don't realize that there are numerous sources of power besides formal authority, such as expertise, appealing personal qualities, position in key networks, and visibility," says Hill.

Supervisors need to explain this to new managers, and help them identify individuals whose cooperation is essential to their team's or department's work. Hill recommends asking questions such as, "Whose cooperation do you need? Whose compliance? Whose opposition would keep you from accomplishing your work? Who needs your cooperation? What sources of power do you have at your disposal to influence these people?"

To help new managers develop sources of informal power, Hill offers these guidelines:

- Provide beginning managers with plenty of opportunities to regularly broaden their expertise.

- Encourage them to "put themselves in others' shoes" so as to understand constituencies' key concerns and priorities.

- Focus their attention on the "big picture"—how things get done in the organization, and who seems to "make things happen."

Hill has seen a lot of new managers disdain "office politics." But as managerial roles have become more complicated, workplace relationships more interdependent, and resources more scarce, managers increasingly have to figure out how to reconcile competing interests. By teaching them to cultivate and exercise unofficial authority, executives can help them balance these complexities.

Mastering a New Identity

In addition to learning how to accumulate informal power, exercise influence, and balance conflicting interests, a new manager must navigate a profound identity shift. He has to transform himself from someone who performs tasks (a "doer") to someone who must get things done through others (a "people developer"). Hill warns executives not to assume that first-time managers grasp this concept.

"You have to explain it to them," she says, "and reassure them that it's normal to experience difficulty during the transition—that there's nothing wrong with them or the organization. Remembering your own experiences as a new manager can help you have more empathy for someone who's just starting out."

Hill also recommends creating "an environment of psychological safety." In other words, "don't overreact when a manager in her first year on the job makes the inevitable misstep. Coach her instead by talking about the judgment calls she needs to make in her new role. Give her enough autonomy to make mistakes, then support her in learning from those mistakes."

In particular, Hill urges bosses to watch for new managers who aren't asking for help. Many of them don't turn to their bosses for support, she says, because they fear being judged as "stupid" or incompetent. Supervisors should seek out new managers who aren't coming to them voluntarily and avoid punishing those who do make themselves vulnerable by asking for help.

Delegating

Like many other managerial demands, delegating decision making involves complex judgment calls. Executives need to educate new managers on the alternatives and degrees of delegation that come up in the managerial role.

Hill suggests asking questions such as, "Is this a decision you need to make alone? Should it be made by your team, within parameters that you specify? Will you make the decision with advice from team members? Will you and your team make the decision together, through consensus?"

Hill adds: "Also watch for delegation mistakes new managers tend to make—such as delegating too much or too little, and failing to follow up after a task has been delegated." Without follow-up, managers don't get information on how their delegation approach worked out. They also miss the opportunity to give feedback to direct reports to whom they've delegated work.

Focus on Development

Though a new manager's relationship with his or her boss can serve as a springboard for learning, an executive's goal isn't to create an exclusive dependency. Rather, Hill maintains, it's to help managers eventually take charge of their own development. That means encouraging them to build a range of developmental relationships—with current and previous peers, former bosses, and individuals outside the company who can serve as mentors, coaches, and sources of emotional support.

Hill also believes that formal training can play an important role. It provides managers with insight into the company's culture and established processes, as well as opportunities to receive systematic feedback on their performance. Equally important, training enables new managers to "forge developmental relationships with peer managers" who are also attending the sessions. Making these connections can be the first step to cultivating a network of influence in the company.

To encourage the kinds of developmental relationships essential for new managers to succeed, companies must establish a culture characterized by a strong coaching orientation.

"Unfortunately," Hill notes, "many companies don't value managerial development—they have more of a 'sink or swim' mentality."

This is especially the case, says Hill, when economic times are tough: people become far more focused on their company's current financial performance, and learning and development fall by the wayside. And when the economy's in trouble, it's much harder to create an environment of psychological safety within which

Debriefing Linda A. Hill

people can make and learn from mistakes and feel comfortable asking for help.

Companies must always make tradeoffs between current performance and long-term learning. In Hill's experience, the few firms that do value development tend to focus educational efforts on their more senior managers and executives.

Countervailing Forces

But attitudes toward managerial development seem to be changing. Hill notes that recent research suggests that lower- and mid-level managers play a far more crucial role in a company's performance than previously assumed. And despite pressures to cut costs, many firms are accepting the idea that the key to surviving highly competitive times is talent, in the form of high performers who also feel deeply committed to their companies. This is particularly true as companies become larger and more complex while also needing to "get more out of fewer employees," she notes.

Perhaps not surprisingly, as companies become more complicated, so, too, does the managerial role. Hill cites an example: "A new manager today may discover his first day on the job that he has to lead a virtual new-product team—something that was rare in earlier decades."

With complexity growing on many different levels, Hill feels certain that the business case for investing in managerial development is much clearer now than before.

"But that doesn't mean that changing a company's culture is easy," she warns.

For this reason, support for a developmental culture has to come from the top. Executives at the highest levels must model the behavior they want to see lower-level managers demonstrate. They also need to establish systems that reinforce a development mentality.

Hill has heard many bosses say that they don't feel they'll be rewarded—financially or otherwise—for coaching and developing their own direct reports. Instead, their companies tend to show more appreciation for short-term, hard-core financial performance.

By tying at least some portion of compensation to managerial development, companies can send the message that they value learning at all levels.

Reprint U0309E

Pulling Yourself Up Through the Ranks

• • •

Loren Gary

Tim Smith, a first-level manager at Boeing, knows a thing or two about leading during times of constant change. What with the downsizing that has intensified in the two years since September 11, he's gone from supervising engineers to supervising hourly employees, and he is currently on a special assignment that involves consolidating operations and relocating them into smaller plants both inside and outside the company. And he's had five different managers in the past 14 months.

To help turn the challenges he's facing into occasions for learning and to further his own development as a leader, Smith is participating in Boeing's Waypoint Project. Established in 2000, this 10-year initiative brings together 120 volunteers from all levels of management in a joint exploration that seeks to turn their trial-by-fire experiences into an intentional process for improving leadership capabilities while accomplishing business objectives. At a time when training dollars are increasingly scarce, Boeing is taking a fresh look at leadership development. There is much to learn from what the leaders of the Waypoint Project and other leadership-development experts have found.

Staff from the Boeing Leadership Center (BLC) interview the volunteers throughout the year. Their findings are made available to all Boeing managers through an interactive Web site, which also allows them to take assessment tests, devise personal development plans, and identify training and stretch assignments.

Participating in Waypoint is not only giving Smith access to a valuable body of knowledge, it is also helping him to identify key development goals. To stay sharp in his current operational responsibilities, he's taking classes on accelerated improvement that will enable him to maintain his certification as an instructor in lean management principles. And to position himself for higher-level management jobs, he's taking a 200-hour course on program management at George Washington University and a two-week course to learn more about strategic leadership.

What puts the Waypoint Project at the cutting edge of leadership training in large organizations? With development programs coming under increased pressure to help an organization achieve or maintain competitive excellence, many organization-directed "push" programs have been found wanting. In such programs, the company selects a relatively small number of managers who have been deemed to possess the greatest leadership potential, gives them access to special educational and networking opportunities, rotates them through a series of high-level assignments, and carefully monitors their progress.

> "With all leadership development, the real driver is the work itself."

But these push programs can turn into little more than credentialing exercises when the participants aren't fully committed to the learning. Consequently, best-practice companies are combining traditional push programs with self-directed "pull" approaches, in which the individual has a high degree of choice and flexibility and thus is more responsible for his own development. The Waypoint Project is Boeing's innovative attempt to create tools to support such self-directed learning. And by making the insights it generates available to all managers, the company hopes to institutionalize the lessons learned from crucible leadership experiences.

A closer examination of Boeing's initiatives, combined with insights from experts about the state of leadership development programs in big companies, yields valuable recommendations both for managers who are looking to develop their direct reports' leadership potential and for those who are trying to plot their own career trajectories.

1: Focus on the job, not the classroom

"With all leadership development, the real driver is the work itself," says James M. Hunt, associate professor of organizational behavior at Babson College. "The learning takes place through challenging assignments."

Interviews with Waypoint participants certainly bear this out: they reveal that 80% of a leader's development occurs through on-the-job activities and experiences, not in the classroom. In particular, says Paul Yost, manager of leadership research at the BLC, the research highlighted 16 critical events in a leader's development, among them turning a unit or group around, starting a business from scratch, making the transition from a line position to a staff position (or vice versa), dealing with a problem employee, and handling your own mistakes or failures. The project's intranet includes a database of insight and advice from managers who've been through these experiences.

2: Look for the overlap between individual interest and the company's strategic needs

"Your leadership development efforts must be driven by the business strategy," says Mary Mannion-Plunkett, senior manager for research, evaluation, and communications at the BLC. "If the business units see the development activities as being separate from the work of accomplishing unit objectives, they're not going to follow through with them."

But one of the fundamental insights of adult education, experts say, is that you won't get anywhere if you try to teach people things they're not interested in. The way to resolve this tension between the goals of the individual and those of the organization is to look for the areas of overlap. The BLC's Waypoint site enables managers to develop personalized development plans that do just this. After reading about the competencies needed for handling a particular position or crucible experience, the manager can choose the ones she's most interested in working on and then find recommendations on how to acquire them.

Even so, the manager's motivation "can be very pragmatic," says Babson's Hunt, who is coauthor with

James R. Weintraub of *The Coaching Manager: Developing Top Talent in Business*. "Some of the things people need to learn in order to be leaders or to rise to a higher-paying position—for example, how to handle conflict—may not be things that they love to do."

3: Remember that companies are dynamic—and so are the leadership skills they require

"It doesn't make much sense to try to define all the competencies of the ideal leader and then map out a rigid development process for acquiring them," says the BLC's Yost. "Markets and technologies change too fast for that to work." Instead, start by identifying the leadership skills that are likely to become more significant in your company in the years ahead. Entrepreneurial thinking skills, for example, are always important, but they're becoming even more so at Boeing in recent years as aircraft sales have declined and the company has sought to identify more services that it can provide to both the commercial and military markets.

Take a broad-minded view of your company's strategic objectives and what skills are needed to accomplish them. For example, think about the circumstances under which it makes sense to let direct reports pursue interests that are not mainstream now but may well be so later on.

4: Know when to reach out

For all the advantages of pull programs, there are still times when push programs are invaluable. "When a manager is moving from one level to another or across functions, or just after a merger, when an organization is trying to blend two cultures—we find that during such times of transition, it's very important for us to be reaching out to people via push programs," says Mannion-Plunkett.

In addition, the Waypoint Project's research has identified six indicators that a manager needs a training "push" to keep his career on course. They include not seeking out job assignments that push him to the edge of his comfort zone, avoiding high-stakes assignments, not building networks and relationships internally and externally, and focusing on near-term performance goals to the exclusion of learning goals. Boeing's training programs for executives include discussions of how to avoid such potential career derailments—and how to help direct reports avoid them, too.

5: Now more than ever, you need to take responsibility for your own development

Push programs for high-potential managers still constitute the core of most firms' leadership development efforts, but a study of Fortune 200 companies by management professors Jon Briscoe of Northern Illinois University and Brooke Derr of Brigham Young University reveals that today there's a much greater degree of individual awareness and involvement in the development process. "At the lower echelons, for managers up to about age 38, there's lots more experimentation and self-directed learning opportunities than before," says Derr, coeditor with Sylvie Roussillon and Frank Bournois of *Cross-Cultural Approaches to Leadership Development*. But push programs for high potentials, which tend to kick in at around age 40, also have more of a pull element than they used to, he adds: "There's a lot of explicit contracting with the high potentials to make sure that the top leadership track is still something they want."

Fewer people are included in push programs these days, says Derr. To get noticed, aspiring managers have to take advantage of the development opportunities that the company provides. The good news is that the metrics for assessing leadership potential are much more transparent now. Says Derr, "Companies are much more likely to spell out what you need to do in order to make it into the future leaders group."

Reprint U0310B

Taking Charge Fast

• • •

Eric McNulty

It is disruptive, expensive, and preventable—yet most executives don't even think about it. It is the mishandled management transition.

The average executive will take on a new role every two to three years. In each job change, it will take more than six months for the executive to go from being a net consumer of corporate value to a net producer. Consider the number of transitions at any medium-size or large company, and the compounded suboptimal performance from key players becomes an enormous value-sucking drain.

Not a particularly heartening picture. And one an increasing number of organizations are taking note of.

For better or worse, companies have become more like sports teams: they expect to bring in individual stars who can have an impact on performance almost immediately. And so there is added pressure these days on executives moving into new roles to get themselves quickly out of the red and into the black.

And if executives need any more motivation to get up to speed very fast, they should know that the actions taken during their first three months, says Harvard Business School professor Michael Watkins, largely determine whether they will succeed over both the short and long term. In his book, *The First 90 Days: Critical Success Strategies for New Leaders at All Levels*, Watkins explores the many vulnerabilities of an incoming leader and presents tactics that can mitigate them, along with strategies for building positive momentum in the critical phases of a transition. Watkins's work and that of other experts suggests that there are four key elements of any successful leadership transition.

1: Craft a Learning Plan

To Watkins, transition failures often result from the "sink or swim" mentality many firms possess. He recommends that a new leader be proactive and develop a formal learning plan well before the first day on the job.

It should include markets, products, customers, technologies, systems, and structures, as well as culture and politics.

"Getting acquainted with a new organization can be like drinking from a fire hose," says Watkins. "You have to focus, take responsibility, and be systematic about deciding what you need to learn and how you will learn it most effectively."

Look to a wide range of information sources in order to get the most complete and accurate picture of your situation. Start with your immediate boss, direct reports, and peers in other departments, but be sure to include salespeople, suppliers, customers, analysts, distributors, and frontline staff as well. Also look for those people who facilitate cross-functional integration and "old timers" who may be unofficial company historians. With each person or group of people, have a clearly defined objective.

2: Promote Yourself

When Georgia Nardi (at their request, the names of the three individuals whose stories we present here have been changed) was promoted to CFO of a half-billion-dollar company in the Midwest, she saw it as a major career accomplishment. She stepped into the role with enthusiasm and was able to complete a critical short-term project successfully. Not long after, however, the people who had promoted her started asking themselves if they had made a mistake. Nardi was acquiring a reputation as unresponsive and disorganized.

Had Nardi somehow hid these traits before her promotion? Had they picked the wrong person? No, but the managers who promoted her *had* made a big mistake. They were so eager to have Nardi take on that crucial short-term assignment that they promoted her before finding her replacement. Thus Nardi had been trying to fulfill both her new responsibilities and her old. Playing "hero" almost cost her her job.

This is a common misstep, says Watkins. You must promote yourself—create a clear line of demarcation between your old role and your new one—for your own mental clarity as well as to set the right expectations for your boss, your peers, and your direct reports. In order to succeed in the new position, he says, you must fully embrace it, and that means letting go of the past.

3: Look Out for Sacred Cows

When Alistair Greenfield was brought in to grow a start-up business unit for a large manufacturer, he found an unsustainable business model, so he quickly developed a clear, if difficult, action plan to bring that news to corporate. His findings were not well received in the unit, nor was the critical feedback that he gave to one of the support staff.

"I didn't understand the informal power structure," says Greenfield. "I needed to make tough decisions and deliver less than pleasant news to my new corporate management. The administrator I critiqued was a long-time employee of the company who was very wired in at the highest levels, despite being far down the hierarchy. She had the power to undermine me while I was still building my credibility."

Unwritten rules, deeply entrenched corporate mythology, and powerful informal networks all are potential minefields for the uninitiated. That's why it's crucial to build relationships and coalitions right from the start.

> It's crucial to build relationships and coalitions right from the start.

Greenfield's tenure was brief, but he walked away with a valuable lesson. "In my next position, I began working on relationships immediately," he says. "I sought out opportunities to help people so that I, in turn, could turn to them for help."

According to Elizabeth McAloon, a New York City–based executive coach, "it really helps to have someone on your side who can help you effectively—and objectively—decode and digest the flood of information, experiences, and emotions that surface during the early stages of transition. All of this unfolds against the backdrop of relationship building—a substantial piece of any successful transition."

4: Build the Team You Need

When Max Miller was promoted into a plant-management position for a midsize company in the South, he faced what can be the most difficult situation for a new leader: the realization that the leadership team he inherited would have to go. Like Greenfield, Miller entered his new role with high hopes: he was promoted within his company to run an operation that had a history of strong financial results. Before starting the position, he didn't probe deeply and assumed that if corporate knew of problems, they would tell him.

Within a week he had realized that the team did not have the skills needed for the job ahead and that there was a serious misalignment of values between the team and the company. Because the financial results had been so strong (thanks to one large, profitable customer that was "locked in"), these underlying problems had gone unnoticed at corporate. Complicating the situation was the defensiveness of the unit's HR people—they were afraid of being blamed for the situation.

Christy Williams of RHR International, a Denver-based consulting firm that works with companies on culture and leadership issues, says there are two lessons to be learned here. "First, you have to treat an internal promotion just as if you were coming in from outside. Ask the tough questions. Tour the facilities. Talk to customers. Second, don't assume that you have to make things work with the existing cast of characters. You might be inheriting someone else's baggage and you don't want to wait 18 months to deal with it."

"Building the right team and securing early wins are two critical building blocks for a successful transition," Watkins says. "In this case, Miller seems to have been wise to act decisively, although a good rule of thumb is to allow 90 days before you decide who will stay and who will go. This allows time to evaluate each individual, test their judgment, let them adjust to you, and see how they will fit into your plan for getting the business where you need it to go."

It is important to remember that you are not the only one in transition. Your new boss, your former boss (if you have moved internally), your direct reports, and people in related departments are all affected.

And these are people whose input and trust you need. You weren't hired or promoted because you have all the answers. Even if you have a lot of them, people have a fundamental need to see that they are respected before they will fully agree to be led. Trust and influence don't automatically come with the position.

Transitions are both an exciting and difficult time. Both the company and the new leader have a tremendous amount invested in a successful transition, and by managing that investment actively and strategically, each can dramatically increase the chances for success.

Reprint U0311B

Succeeding Ms. (Mr.) Wonderful

• • •

Jennifer McFarland

A leader's fundamental responsibility, says Jim Collins, author of *Good to Great*, "is to ensure that her successor is even more successful in the next generation than she was. Period."

If that's so, then many leaders—especially many of the most revered ones—have shirked their responsibility. How else to explain the accepted wisdom that instead of being the person who follows a beloved leader, you want to be the one who comes after the person who follows the beloved leader?

Making the transition to a new leadership role is difficult enough; replacing a legend can intensify the challenge. "People who have been led by someone great are going to inevitably go through a grieving process," says Michael Watkins, associate professor at Harvard Business School. "There's no replacing that person and you shouldn't even bother trying." Easy for him to say. The on-the-ground reality, however, often makes it hard to avoid the trap of trying to emulate your predecessor. After all, everybody adored her—wouldn't you want them to adore you, too?

Well, snap out of it. Sure, succeeding a much-admired leader can have its advantages. It can also be a minefield of unspoken expectations. Fail to uncover and address them in accordance with your own mandate and you'll find yourself being hoist with those petards. Some tips for defusing a potentially incendiary situation:

Assess the Revered Leader's Legacy

"Do your homework," says Michael Sanders, director of client development at Staub Leadership Consultants. "Talk to whomever you're replacing" before your first day on the new job. Otherwise, you may not "learn what you need to know to make sound early decisions, leading to judgments that damage your credibility," writes Watkins in his workbook *Taking Charge in Your New Leadership Role*. Ask the outgoing leader to talk about her legacy—her accomplishments and the reputation she's built for her business. Ask her to describe her managerial style and to evaluate her team. This will help you uncover not only the problem areas but also the beloved leader's secrets for handling particular situations and personalities in your new work environment.

Ask similar questions of the people who will be your peers and direct reports. What aspects of your predecessor's legacy do they admire most, and why? How did she behave in bad times? What were her shortcomings? You won't receive direct, expansive answers to all these questions; even so, you'll be able to infer a great deal from what you do get. Above all you'll gain an understanding of what type of leader your predecessor was. That understanding will help you diagnose the situation you're entering.

The Genius with a Thousand Helpers and the Level 5 Leader

A Tale of Two Drugstore Chains

Jack Eckerd, architect of the Eckerd's empire, "had a genius for picking the right stores to buy," writes Jim Collins in *Good to Great*. By contrast, Cork Walgreen, founder of the Walgreen's chain, "had a genius for picking the right people to hire. Whereas Jack Eckerd had a gift for seeing which store should go in what locations, Cork Walgreen had a gift for seeing which people should go in what seats." Eckerd failed at choosing a successor—"the single most important decision facing any executive," notes Collins. "Without his guiding

(continued)

The Genius with a Thousand Helpers and the Level 5 Leader

genius, Eckerd's company began a long decline, eventually being acquired by J.C. Penney." But Walgreen "developed multiple outstanding candidates and selected a superstar successor, who may prove to be even better than Cork himself."

Eckerd is typical of what Collins calls "the genius with 1,000 helpers." Companies headed by such leaders tend to have "a bunch of capable helpers assembled to assist the great genius" instead of a genuine executive team. The guidance mechanism for corporate strategy tends to reside inside the genius's head, not in the "group dialogue and shared insights" of the executive team. Walgreen personifies what Collins calls "the Level 5 leader." Such an individual "blends extreme personal humility with intense professional will." Whereas the genius with 1,000 helpers tackles the issue of *what to do* first, for the Level 5 leader the issue of *who are the right people* to put on the executive team comes first.

Funny thing is, leaders are often revered for very different reasons. Employees can develop a great fondness for either type described here. Don't take the fact that people admire your predecessor as proof that she's attained Level 5 sainthood. You'll have to probe deeper to ascertain which type of leader you're succeeding. And probe you must: the legacy you inherit and the actions you'll need to take will depend on what you uncover.

Compare the Legacy to Your Mandate

Why were you chosen as the replacement? What were you brought in to do? Your new direct reports may see your mission as sustaining the success that's already been achieved, but your charge from the people you'll be reporting to may be quite different. For one thing, the fiscal or economic forecast may be shifting dramatically. Instead of merely staying the course, you may need to chart entirely new directions for your group. It's also possible that there are underlying problems with your new unit's performance. The respect your predecessor commanded or her very affability may have made it easy for senior management to overlook these concerns, but you've been tasked with taking them on. The assumption here is that you've already decided you're up to the challenge of reconciling any tension between your predecessor's legacy and the way forward; if that's the case, your next step is clear.

Spell Out Your Mandate

This can be difficult when your mandate is to shake up the status quo. When David Maxwell became CEO of Fannie Mae, the company was losing $1 million every business day. Clearly, Fannie Mae needed a new strategy.

But Maxwell, manifesting what Collins calls Level 5 leadership behavior, knew that the *who* was more important than the *what*—in other words, that the people issues needed to take precedence over the strategy. "David sat down with every single person and personally interviewed them, then he observed their track record," says Collins. "He basically said, 'Look, I want you to think about how demanding this is going to be. If you don't think you're going to like it, that's fine. Nobody's going to hate you.' Maxwell made it absolutely clear that there would only be seats for A players who were going to put forth A+ effort, and that people who weren't up for it had better get off the bus now."

Carefully delineate any differences between your standards and those of your predecessor. Help your unit understand how these standards flow from the challenges you've been hired to address. When the inevitable "But she always did it this way" comment surfaces, the temptation to acquiesce and copy the behavior of your beloved predecessor will be strong. Try to turn the temptation into an opportunity to describe your own leadership style with as much specificity as you can.

Get the Right People on Board

Consider the contribution or presence of every person in your new group. Who's on your bus? Who should be in which seat? A common pitfall, writes Watkins, is to "retain subordinates with a record of mediocre performance in the belief that your leadership will make a difference." The result: you "waste precious time and energy trying to compensate for the team's weaknesses." Give subordinates a chance to get on board with the program and to conform to the new standards. But don't wait too long to decide that some people need to be moved off the bus.

Then, too, don't be surprised if some people voluntarily get off the bus. Sanders did that himself once. "I've never quit a job and felt so good about it in my life—because I was in control," he says. As a result of the experience, Sanders advises his clients to extend the same offer to their direct reports. "I would tell them that I would understand if any of them felt that they couldn't work under those conditions. You invite them to disengage," he says. "They need to feel good about that decision, and a good leader can help them do that. I'd encourage supervisors to spend time with these people trying to work it out. But you always want to end up with their dignity intact, so they know that they are valuable human beings."

Obviously, you'd rather that events not take this course, "which is why inside leaders correlate with much better results than leaders brought in from the outside," says Collins. It's tough to see capable people opt for the exit ramp, and then to have to find and train replacements for them. But in the end, only those who are willing to carry out your mandate will deliver value.

For Further Reading

Good to Great: Why Some Companies Make the Leap . . . and Others Don't by Jim Collins (2001, HarperBusiness)

Taking Charge in Your New Leadership Role: A Workbook by Michael Watkins (2001, Harvard Business School Publishing)

Reprint U0110B

Making the
Best Decisions

. . .

For new and experienced leaders alike, decision making has grown more complicated than ever. Leaders must make choices quickly—often with scant information at hand. As you discover in this section's articles, leaders need to master new decision-making skills in order to keep pace and make the wisest choices for their companies. For example, you'll want to develop a greater tolerance for ambiguity and be willing to constantly reinvent the way your teams operate. You'll also want to gather more input on key decisions from people at every level of your organization, as well as learn how to quickly assess the reasons behind a decision before taking the plunge and implementing it.

Three Skills for Today's Leaders

• • •

Leadership is one of the most heavily studied subjects in the literature on management, yet it remains elusive. What is leadership? What does a leader do? What skills turn a manager into a leader? These are difficult questions, particularly since leadership itself is changing. But there are some new attempts at answers.

In 1999, for example, management thinkers and executives from the private and nonprofit sectors gathered at a conference convened by the Center for Creative Leadership (CCL), a think tank in Greensboro, NC. The goal was to examine current leadership practices and needs. Participants focused on the fact that changing conditions in many organizations require leaders to develop new skills and perspectives.

One such change: the rapid pace of decision making. Quick, easily available information allows companies (and their competitors) to move with extraordinary speed. As a consequence, CEOs and leadership teams are hard pressed to sift information and make decisions with due haste. "One of the purposes of leadership is to step back and find patterns and meaning in all the accumulation of data and opinions and conflict," says John Alexander, CCL's president. "But you have to do it under enormous pressure these days."

How can leaders find patterns in the chaos, articulate action plans, communicate them clearly throughout the organization—and do it all quickly enough? Management researchers and writers at the CCL conference focused on three key skills.

Handling Ambiguity

Today, the shape of markets is unclear, the right moves for a company are hard to assess, and it's all going to change soon anyway. This alters the nature of leadership.

In a more stable marketplace, a leader could be seen as a visionary, divining the future—or as a sage commander able to give detailed marching orders to the troops. Those models of leadership no longer work. Leaders now

> ## Most executives regard crises and surprises as signs of inept leadership.

must be willing to tolerate ambiguity, and to act even when the future is murky. No one can give detailed marching orders to the troops, because no one can be sure where the troops are headed.

If the ability to tolerate uncertainty is an essential skill of leadership, it's a skill that's in short supply, says Randy White, a social psychologist who formerly headed CCL's executive development programs. "Often when you talk about leadership deficits, people will point to the leader's difficulty in dealing with ambiguity and uncertainty." But White, now a principal of Executive Development Group and an adjunct professor at Duke University's Fuqua School of Business, has developed a tool for assessing people's ability to handle ambiguity—it's called the Ambiguity Architect—and believes that the skill can be taught. For instance, if the assessment shows that a manager tends to steer clear of projects with difficult solutions, she might be encouraged to examine how a peer successfully handled such a project. Then she could ask to be assigned a tough task to build her skills in this kind of situation.

Managing the System

Complex systems such as large corporations aren't linear; rather, they're networks of multiple connections and relationships. So executives who try to manage in linear fashion—begin with business strategy, follow with product development, production, marketing, and sales, all in order—are underestimating their task. And management fads that aim a magic bullet at one aspect of a company or its people ignore the reality of complexity. For instance, companies that tried to reengineer deeply embedded systems often found parts of those systems mysteriously reappearing. "The huge popularity and subsequent collapse of the reengineering movement was almost a tribute to [the shortcomings of] the old linear thinking," declares David Hurst, a visiting fellow at CCL who is also a research fellow at the University of Western Ontario's National Centre for Management Research and Development. "The whole notion of starting with a clean sheet, which was one of the icons of reengineering, is ludicrous in complex systems."

Hurst draws on recent findings from fields such as cognitive science and parallel computing to paint a different picture of organizations. Business development, he argues, typically begins with explosive, unfettered growth, followed by the introduction of management systems to guide the company's energies. But the organizational life cycle doesn't end there. Crisis and renewal are integral parts of organizational development; companies invent new ways of doing things in response to unexpected challenges. This kind of rejuvenation is healthy, since the alternative is organizational death. Yet most executives regard crises and surprises as signs of poor planning and inept leadership.

So what should a leader do? Ride and guide organizational change rather than hinder it. Create crises. Hurst uses the metaphor of "controlled burn," the process by which forest managers burn small sections to clear deadwood, thereby heading off uncontrollable wildfires that would destroy the whole shebang. Business leaders, similarly, should prune their organizations and force new growth rather than allowing stagnation. Jack Welch won fame for shaking up General Electric in the early 1980s by demanding that each GE business had to become No. 1 or No. 2 in its market. But he continued to launch a new internal revolution every few years after that. Ultimately each GE unit had a full-time "destroyyourbusiness.com" team charged with reinventing the group's way of managing, operating, even thinking.

Learning Group Leadership

Companies today are turning themselves inside out to increase their agility. Some push decision making down so that employees in the field can be more responsive to customers. Others give teams responsibility for their own work. So-called learning organizations try to tap the insights and intelligence of employees at all levels. All these innovative arrangements stand the usual notion of leadership on its head: authority is no longer concentrated in a few people at the top of the ladder.

This shift in the number and nature of leaders highlights a truth about the whole concept of leadership, argues CCL senior fellow Bill Drath: leadership is a natural property of social systems. People joining organizations enter into implicit contracts about their roles. In this sense, he says, "everyone in a company is a participant in leadership." The implication: leadership is as much a function of a company's social systems as it is a quality in individuals. Improving a company's leadership and decision making is a matter of improving organizational processes, not simply hiring a more forceful CEO.

What does this mean in practice? Drath works as a consultant to companies with leadership difficulties, and often finds a key problem to be "communication gridlock" among managers. For example, at a large telecommunications company challenged by the need to respond to external change, "most of their meetings are about making a decision or problem solving—before they've arrived at a mutual understanding of the problem. Right away they get into difficulty, because everybody is advocating for a particular solution without understanding the range of viewpoints." Drath's prescription: a "mediated dialogue" to improve the managers' communication; the group talks about separate pieces of the market landscape one at a time, slowly building consensus on the overall picture.

This discussion technique improves the whole management team's capacity for leadership. "You've heard of decision-making support systems," Drath says. "We're looking at what comes before that. What we're trying to develop is 'sense-making' support systems."

For Further Reading

"The Ambiguity Architect: Navigating Rough Water," version 9.1, by Randall P. White, Philip Hodgson, et al. (1999, Lominger Limited)

The Future of Leadership: Riding the Corporate Rapids into the 21st Century by Randall P. White, Philip Hodgson, and Stuart Crainer (1996, Pitman Publishing)

Crisis and Renewal by David K. Hurst (1995, Harvard Business School Press)

"Changing Our Minds about Leadership" by Wilfred H. Drath, in *Issues and Observations* (1996, Center for Creative Leadership)

Reprint U9911A

What Leaders Allow Themselves to Know

• • •

Paul Michelman

How could Julius Caesar have been blind to the warnings about his imminent fall even as they fell like hail upon him? Why didn't Compaq CEO Eckhard Pfeiffer listen to the senior managers who urged him time and again to pay attention to the upstart PC makers who were siphoning off Compaq's customers? How is it that former *New York Times* executive editor Howell Raines continued to engage in the very behaviors that had alienated

What Leaders Allow Themselves to Know

an entire newsroom even after a 17,000-word article in the *New Yorker* made his problems as plain as a five-column headline?

According to leadership scholar Warren Bennis, to comprehend the curious actions—or inactions—taken by these leaders in the face of turbulence, we must first look at the way they dealt with the information available to them, specifically "what they allowed themselves to know and when they allowed themselves to know it."

> "The tragedy is how we lose good people because they cannot listen or don't want to listen."

Bennis, who is a Distinguished Professor of Business Administration at the University of Southern California and also holds advisory roles at Harvard Business School and Harvard's Kennedy School of Government, has been reshaping our perceptions of leadership for five decades. He recently sat down with *Harvard Management Update* to discuss his thinking about the way leaders process information. His ideas provide a framework for understanding decision making by looking at how and

165

why our minds accept or reject certain information, particularly disconfirming information.

The Barriers to Better Decisions

We all employ filters, Bennis says, that direct the flow of information in our minds. These filters govern which data lands on the active agenda of our consciousness and which gets shuttled off to the mind's dark corners. "For a variety of reasons, the mind doesn't give you license to interpret certain data," he says. "You don't deal with the issues that you don't want to believe are real, and this leaves you with a skewed vision." Could that explain, Bennis asks, why the White House plowed ahead with making its case for war in Iraq when hindsight suggests officials should have seen that some data used to build the justification was not airtight? Did the president's passionate belief that the White House's plan was right for the country allow information that supported his preconceptions to trump disconfirming data?

If so, Bush's decision-making process illustrates one of the three filters Bennis has identified as governing the flow of data into the conscious mind: *social filters*. These are filters that allow leaders to reject certain data by simply not paying attention to its source. "When I was in Abu Dhabi a couple of years ago, a colleague there told me about a Middle Eastern phrase used in describing people who stop listening," Bennis says. "He called it 'tired ears.'"

Think about Pfeiffer, who led nearly seven years of uninterrupted growth at Compaq before things took a profound turn for the worse. "He had an A list and a B list," Bennis says. "And his A list said, 'Yes, sir,' 'Aye, aye, sir'" to whatever strategy Pfeiffer would proffer. "But the B list was saying, 'Hey, boss, you know maybe we better look at what Gateway's doing or what Dell is doing because they're taking away a lot of our customers.' Pfeiffer didn't listen to or look at the evidence. Eventually, he just stopped seeing the people on the B list who were giving him disconfirming, bad news. He had tired ears."

So did Pfeiffer deliberately put himself in a position in which certain information couldn't reach him because he wanted to avoid dealing with what he *knew* was true? Not necessarily, Bennis says. It's possible he simply began to ignore any data that did not affirm what he *believed*, on some level, to be true. It's important to distinguish that kind of blindness to information from the legal concept of *willful blindness*, in which an individual purposely closes himself off to data in order to create ignorance-by-design of certain facts—for instance, what former Enron CEO Kenneth Lay may have engaged in. The forces at work here are often of a less conscious and purposeful nature.

Look, too, Bennis says, at Shakespeare's Caesar. The evidence screams danger. "His wife dreams of him as a bleeding statue with 100 spouts and lusty Romans washing their hands in his blood. An owl hooted, which meant a lot in 44 B.C. Rome. A lion ran through the streets."

But Caesar ignored the signs at every turn. He wouldn't even accept the note warning about Cassius, Casca, and Brutus that Artemidorus tried repeatedly to give him. "Why is it that he didn't pay attention?" Bennis asks. The same question could be asked about Pfeiffer, Raines, and countless others who have encountered great leadership failures, he says. "The tragedy is how we lose good people because they cannot listen or don't want to listen."

If social filters allow us shut out particular sources of information, *contextual filters* let us reject the significance of our surroundings. To explain, Bennis turns to his own experiences as president of the University of Cincinnati from 1971 to 1978. "I was brought in to rattle the cages and to make that city-supported school into a major state university," he says. "Here I was, a kind of foreigner, and the people in Cincinnati thought I was stealing the university away from them." So the 80-something Fred Lazurus Jr., founder of Federated Department Stores, offered what Bennis describes as wise counsel. "He said, 'Warren, this is a real conservative city. Don't be too visible. Work with your faculty, work with your students. Don't get sucked into the limelight.'"

But Bennis didn't really try to understand the culture he was dealing with, and when his saber rattling at the university caught the attention of the press, he didn't exactly play the role of shrinking violet. *Cincinnati Magazine*, for instance, wrote a profile that made Bennis, his work, and his family "look like Camelot," he says. "I kind of enjoyed it." He was even talked into hosting a local television program called *Bennis!*

Not surprisingly, those highly visible trappings of leadership did not always sit well with the constituencies whose support Bennis's mission required, making his role as change agent all that more difficult.

"Here's the lesson about context," Bennis says. "I didn't take the time to understand the city—its pride, its history. I didn't take time to honor it."

Consider another leader brought in to effect change: Hewlett-Packard's Carly Fiorina. "There were three strikes against her to begin with," Bennis says. "She's a woman, not an engineer, and the first non-Hewlett-Packard person ever to be elevated to the top level. How does she navigate between the past and the present?"

What Fiorina has done is carefully use symbols of HP's rich tradition in spelling out her vision of the future. For example, she initially employed the image of Dave Packard and Bill Hewlett as the boys in the garage to create excitement for how HP would continue to generate groundbreaking ideas. The awareness of the situation that Fiorina displayed allowed her to remove the contextual filters that may have led her to a different, less effective approach to communicating her vision for HP.

The third and final filter that Bennis identifies is governed by *self-knowledge*: what you know and don't know about yourself. To explain, Bennis turns again to his own experience.

"For a lot of reasons, some having to do with ambition, some having to do with wanting to see whether my ideas really had validity on the ground, I had the desire to be a university president," Bennis says. "I wanted to be

> A lack of "self-knowledge is the most common, everyday source of leadership failures," Bennis says.

one so bad that I left my MIT job, where I had what every professor dreams of—a corner office, tenure at a great institution—and I took a job as provost at SUNY Buffalo." Four years in Buffalo then led to the opportunity that Bennis had been waiting for, a university presidency at Cincinnati.

After seven years at the helm of the university, Bennis delivered a speech at the Harvard Graduate School of Education on the leadership role of a university president. "I worked very hard on the talk, and I thought it went really well," he recalls. "And then I took Q&A."

From the back of the room, Paul Ylvisacker, then dean of Harvard's Graduate School of Education, floated what Bennis describes as "a real knuckleball" of a question: " 'Warren, do you *love* being president of the University of Cincinnati? Do you love being president?' I was totally stumped. . . . But I finally was able to look up at him and say, 'Paul, I don't know.' "

Later, on the plane back to Cincinnati, Bennis realized "what it was that Paul was picking up in my eyes," he says. It was that Bennis's heart was not in being president—he just didn't have the passion. He realized later, he says, that being a university president was "not my calling."

As a result of Ylvisacker's question, Bennis was forced to confront his lack of self-knowledge and, in doing so, was able to make a decision that was very different from the one he had made a decade earlier. In effect, he had gained a greater level of control by opening up the filter governed by self-knowledge.

When leaders lack self-knowledge, Bennis says, their decision-making capabilities are compromised. No matter what information is available to you, if you don't know yourself—what drives you to do what you do—the likelihood of misinterpreting and misusing that data increases dramatically.

A lack of "self-knowledge is the most common, *everyday* source of leadership failures," Bennis says. "A lot of gifted individuals I've known over the years who found themselves leading organizations aspired to that top position without knowing what it entailed and what was in store for them. They wanted to *be* a CEO but didn't want to *do* a CEO's job. That's the first question I ask all 'high-potential' leaders. Do you know what's in store, and do you know if the role fits your skill set and/or your 'best self?' That's exactly what I didn't ask myself."

Pursuing the "Full Spectrum" of Data

Building a greater base of knowledge about one's circumstances is the critical element in eliminating the role of all three of the filters Bennis identifies. Harking back to the story of Caesar, Bennis wrote in his column for *CIO Insight* magazine, "Wise leaders know to beware not the ides of March, but the likelihood that their power will isolate them." They then take action to guard against that isolation, he says, both before and after making decisions. When Clark Clifford took over the Defense Department from Robert McNamara during the war in Vietnam, "he began talking to people at every level of the organization, not just the direct reports, not just getting the usual news," Bennis says. "FedEx CIO Robert Carter holds frequent town-hall meetings with his staff and cultivates candor by sharing a meal every month with eight employees," he writes.

Bennis urges leaders to take that strategy one step further by engaging in decision-making postmortems that give leadership teams the opportunity to revisit the reasoning behind a decision before a plan of action is implemented. After the members of the GE board had come to an agreement to name Jeff Immelt to succeed Jack Welch, for example, the board took three weeks—on Welch's recommendation—to let the decision sit before the official vote was taken and an announcement made.

Leaders must always be certain they are accessing the full spectrum of data and opinion, Bennis says. "I think the best leaders find out the way Henry V found out," he notes. On the eve of battle, "he took off his royal robes, put on an enlisted man's army clothes, and he went off and huddled with the troops and asked them what was going on."

Reprint #U0402C

The Perils of Being the Best and the Brightest

· · ·

Robert B. Cialdini

Group consultation has long been lauded as the best process for problem solving in organizations because it results in a wider range of solutions than most individuals can design on their own. Now there's a study, from psychologist Patrick Laughlin and his colleagues at the University of Illinois, that shows that the approaches and outcomes of cooperating groups are not just better than those of the average group member, but are better than even the group's best problem solver functioning alone.

These findings underscore the importance of communication in problem solving and have important implications for managers and anyone else who works as part of a team. Far too often, a leader—who, by virtue of greater experience or wisdom or skill, is deemed the ablest problem solver in a group—fails to ask for input from team members. Equally dangerous, members of a team often relinquish problem-solving responsibilities to the leader and fail to provide her with important information for moving forward on a decision.

The consequences of this vicious circle? Suboptimal solutions, bad choices, wrong directions, and avoidable errors.

Don't Go It Alone

Laughlin's data tells us why even the best problem solver operating individually will be beaten to a demonstrably correct solution by a cooperating unit.

First, the lone problem solver can't match the diversity of knowledge and perspectives of a multiperson unit that includes him. Other members will have had experiences with similar or related problems that will allow the team to recognize fruitful versus fruitless choices more clearly and quickly. Furthermore, this diversity of input can do more than merely add to the storehouse of information that the best problem solver can employ; it can also stimulate thinking processes that would not have developed in wholly internal monologues. We all can recall being led to a productive insight by the comment of a colleague who didn't deliver the insight itself but who sparked an association that did the trick.

Second, the solution seeker who goes it alone loses a significant advantage—the power of parallel processing. Whereas a cooperating unit can distribute the many subtasks of a problem-solving campaign among its members, the lone operator must perform each sequentially. This requirement considerably extends the time spent on the effort. In addition, it strains the capacities and energies of the problem solver because the subtasks often include activities that are daunting in their difficulty (e.g., information integration), time-consuming in their execution (e.g., library/Internet research), and demotivating in their tediousness (e.g., fact checking).

The Nobel Prize–Losing Error

These findings echo a remarkable interview published on the 50th anniversary of the publication of perhaps the most important scientific discovery of our time— that of the double-helix structure of DNA, as revealed in the Nobel Prize–winning work of James Watson and Francis Crick. The interview, with Watson, was designed to inquire into those aspects of the duo's efforts that had led them to solve the problem ahead of an array of highly accomplished rival investigators.

> "If you're the brightest
> person in the room,
> you're in trouble."

At first, Watson ticked off a set of contributory factors that were unsurprising: he and Crick had identified the problem as the most important one to attack. They were passionate about it, devoting themselves single-mindedly to the task. They were willing to try approaches that came from outside their areas of familiarity.

Then he added a stunning reason for their success: he and Crick had cracked the elusive code of DNA because they weren't the most intelligent of the scientists pursuing the answer. According to Watson, the smartest of the lot was Rosalind Franklin, a brilliant British scientist who was working in Paris at the time.

"Rosalind was so intelligent," observed Watson, "that she rarely sought advice. If you're the brightest person in the room, you're in trouble." That comment illuminates a familiar error seen in the actions of many well-intentioned leaders.

Captainitis

Another type of error stems from a failure to collaborate. It's called *captainitis*, and it refers not to the tendency of a leader to assume all problem-solving responsibilities but to the equally regrettable tendency of team members to opt out of responsibilities that are properly theirs.

The error gets its name from the sometimes-deadly type of passivity exhibited by crew members of multi-piloted aircraft when the flight captain makes a clearly wrong-headed decision. Accident investigators have repeatedly registered disastrous instances when even an obvious error made by a captain was not corrected by other crew members.

> The recommendation here isn't to take votes when making hard business determinations. The final decision is properly the leader's alone to make.

Consider the following exchange, recorded on an airliner's flight recorder minutes before it crashed into the Potomac River near Washington National Airport in 1982:

> Copilot: Let's check the ice on those tops [wings] again since we've been sitting here awhile.
> Captain: No. I think we get to go in a minute.
> Copilot: *[Referring to an instrument reading]* That doesn't seem right, does it? Uh, that's not right.
> Captain: Yes, it is. . . .
> Copilot: Ah, maybe it is.
> *[Sound of plane straining unsuccessfully to gain altitude]*
> Copilot: Larry, we're going down!
> Captain: I know it.
> *[Sound of impact that killed the captain, copilot, and 76 others.]*

Captainitis is not limited to air travel. In one study, researchers tested the willingness of well-trained nurses to give up their decision-relevant responsibilities regarding a patient once the "boss" of the case—the attending physician—had spoken. To perform the experiment, one of the researchers made a call to 22 separate nurses' stations on various surgical, medical, pediatric, and psychiatric wards. He identified himself as a hospital physician and directed the answering nurse to give 20 milligrams of the drug Astrogen to a specific ward patient. In 95% of the instances, the nurse went straight to the ward medicine cabinet, secured the ordered dosage of the drug, and started for the patient's room to administer it—even though the drug had not been cleared for hospital use, the prescribed dosage was twice the maximum daily dose set by the manufacturer, and the directive was given by a man the nurse had never met or even talked with before on the phone.

In drawing conclusions from their results, the authors of the hospital study made a telling point. They concluded that in fully staffed medical units like the ones they examined, it is natural to assume that multiple "professional intelligences"—i.e., the doctors', nurses', and assistants'—are working to ensure that the best decisions are made. But in fact, under the conditions of the study, only one of those intelligences—the physicians'—may be functioning.

It appears that the nurses unhooked their considerable professional intelligences in deferring to the doctor. Yet the nurses' actions are understandable. Regarding such matters, the attending physician is both *in* authority and *an* authority.

That is, the doctor is, first of all, in charge and therefore able to sanction noncompliant staffers. Second, the doctor possesses the superior medical training that can lead others to defer automatically to his or her expert status.

Accordingly, we shouldn't be surprised when medical staffers are reluctant to challenge a physician's treatment pronouncements. Nonetheless, we should be more than a little disquieted by this behavior, not just because of the way it could play out during our next hospital visit, but because of the way it could affect any work setting, including our own.

Implications for Leaders

What common lesson flows from the two kinds of errors we have considered? Leaders attacking a knotty problem that possesses an objectively correct solution must collaborate unfailingly with team members toward its resolution—even when they are the best informed or most experienced or ablest of the group. This means setting up systems that ensure collaborative exchanges whether or not the collaboration seems necessary. To do less is a fool's gamble.

But isn't there a different type of gamble that a fully collaborative leader takes? Doesn't this approach risk the notoriously poor outcomes of decision by committee? No.

The recommendation here isn't to employ vote taking or nose counting when making hard business determinations. In fact, the recommendation here isn't for joint decisions at all in such instances. The final decision is properly the leader's alone to make. That's one thing leaders are paid for, typically because they've given evidence of being able to make such choices better than the people who haven't achieved leader status.

However, the key to decision-making success is for the leader to avoid engaging alone in the processes that lead up to the final verdict. It is these predecisional processes that, when jointly undertaken, will benefit the sole decision maker so richly.

If leaders who arrange for regular team input can expect to achieve problem-solving gains, might they also expect to lose something else in the bargain—for instance, subsequent rapport with and input from those whose ideas are rejected? Sometimes members' egos can be bruised and they can feel discouraged if the leader doesn't adopt their proposal or favored course of action.

Fortunately, when inviting cooperative efforts, leaders can take an approach that can generate high levels of collaboration while avoiding this potential problem. From the outset, leaders need to encourage everyone with a stake in the decision process to make a contribution to it and, simultaneously, to assure all concerned that each contribution—while perhaps not the deciding factor—will be a factor in the process.

Thus the leader must make the commitment that, even though many recommendations may not be followed, each is important to optimal decision development and will be given full attention.

That may not sound like much of a commitment, but when properly implemented, it's more than enough.

Reprint C0404A

Communicating Effectively

• • •

Effective communication is the overarching skill that enables new and experienced leaders to get information they need from others to make decisions, convey a compelling vision, and inspire people to do their best. The articles in this section offer basic guidelines for good communication—such as using precise diction and startling facts, clarifying abstractions through analogies, and leavening difficult messages with appropriate humor. Additional communication skills include ensuring that every employee understands your company's philosophy and values, providing direct reports with information to deepen their understanding of the company's strategic direction, and letting employees know that you value their ideas.

Language

Churchill's Key to Leadership

• • •

Nick Wreden

He is quoted as often as Shakespeare and Mark Twain. U.S. presidents from FDR on have used him for inspiration. His words have seeped into everyday language: "finest hour," "blood, toil, tears and sweat," "Iron Curtain," and even "business as usual."

The man, of course, is Winston Churchill, best known for his wartime leadership. As prime minister of Britain, he almost single-handedly rallied the British people to stand up against the Nazi juggernaut. But his entire life was marked by accomplishment, from his participating in the last great cavalry charge of the British Empire to his becoming an honorary citizen of the United States by an act of Congress.

A significant driver of his success was his skill as a communicator. As John F. Kennedy said, "He mobilized the English language and sent it into battle." He served as a journalist in Cuba, India, Sudan, and South Africa; writing fees generated the bulk of his income throughout his life. His articles, speeches, books, and other material totaled an estimated 30 million words. This output was not only solid, but gifted. In 1953, Churchill won the Nobel Prize for Literature.

Churchill recognized the relationship between language and leadership at an early age. At 23, he wrote a treatise on oratory, "The Scaffolding of Rhetoric," that was not published until after his death. It begins: "Of all the talents bestowed upon men, none is so precious as the gift of oratory. He who enjoys it wields a power more durable than that of a great king." In this piece, Churchill identifies the five elements of great speeches: correctness of diction, rhythm, accumulation of argument, analogy, and extravagance of language. Reliance upon these rhetorical workhorses accounts for the strength of Churchill's speeches, and they remain touchstones for any speech today, whether it's delivered at a political rally or at a stockholders' meeting.

1: The Right Words, Nothing More

Churchill writes that "there is no more important element in the technique of rhetoric than the continual employment of the best possible word." He insisted on simplification. He renamed "Local Defense Volunteers" as "Home Guard." Even "aeroplane" was shortened to "plane" by Churchillian fiat.

To encourage precise, economical diction, Churchill allowed his aides to use no more than a single sheet of paper to marshal their arguments.

2: Rhythm Speaks

Rhythm, says Churchill in his essay, requires a "peculiar balance" of phrases that results in a cadence closer to blank verse than to prose. To ensure such rhythm, he initially dictated much of what he wrote. Of his dictation technique, Thomas Montalbo, author of *Public Speaking Made Easy: Magic Keys to Success*, writes in an essay: "He put his ideas to rhetoric as composers set theirs to music. The cigar in his hand served as a baton to punctuate the rhythm of his words. He tested words and phrases; muttering to himself; weighing them; striving to balance his thoughts; making sure the sound, rhythm and harmony were to his liking."

Churchill loved poetry and was able to recite long poems decades after memorizing them. He even wrote his speeches out in psalm style to ensure his phrasing marched to the rhythm of poetry. A 1940 BBC speech about the Nazi menace dances between prose and poetry:

All of them hope that the storm will pass
before their turn comes to be devoured.
　　But I fear—I fear greatly—
　　the storm will not pass.

It will rage and it will roar, ever more loudly,
ever more widely.
　　It will spread to the South;
　　it will spread to the North.

3: Facts to Build On

Next, Churchill advises an accumulation of argument, or a "rapid succession of waves of sound and vivid pictures" that uses facts to bolster a logical conclusion. Later, in *My Early Life*, first published in 1930, he compares writing to building a house: "The foundations have to be laid, the data assembled, and the premises must bear the weight of the conclusions." He read reams of material, including several newspapers, daily and depended heavily on a team of researchers. Confidants both inside and outside the government gave him facts about German rearmament that buttressed many of his speeches about the long-term Nazi threat.

4: Analogies Clarify, Amplify

Churchill was a master of analogy. "Whether [analogies] translate an established truth into simple language or whether they adventurously aspire to reveal the unknown, they are among the most formidable weapons of the rhetorician," he writes in "The Scaffolding of Rhetoric."

He used this elaborate series of analogies to encourage Londoners to bear up under the Blitz:

> Death and sorrow will be the companions of our journey; hardship our garment; constancy and valour our only shield. . . . Our quality and deeds must burn and glow through the gloom of Europe until they become the veritable beacon of its salvation.

5: Speaker and Audience, Mutually Engaged

Finally, Churchill says communicators need a jolt of "wild extravagance." Facts that build the foundation for a logical conclusion are not enough. Both the audience and the speaker must be emotionally engaged. For an audience to cry, the speaker must feel pain; to rouse indignation, a speaker must communicate anger. In 1938, after the fall of Austria to the Nazis, Churchill used these vivid, emotionally charged words to urge England to rearm:

> We should lay aside every hindrance and endeav-
> our by uniting the whole force and spirit of our
> people to raise again a great British nation stand-
> ing up before all the world; for such a nation,
> rising in its ancient vigour, can even at this hour
> save civilisation.

The gifted use of these rhetorical basics undergirds Churchill's oratorical brilliance, but other tools lend their support, including:

Preparation

A friend once said of Churchill: "Winston has spent the best years of his life writing impromptu speeches." A 40-minute speech might take six to eight hours to prepare and practice. Debate in the House of Commons was expected to be give-and-take; reading from a prepared speech was frowned upon. Since improvised oratory was not one of Churchill's strengths, he memorized his speeches, glancing at the prepared manuscript only to jog his memory.

One Speech, One Theme

Despite oratorical flourishes and rolling sentences, Churchill concentrated on a single message in each speech, ending with a call to action. "Too often, speakers will cover a multitude of subjects. Churchill rightly understood that the audience needed to grasp his message without confusion," says Larry Kryske, author of *The Churchill Factor: Creating Your Finest Hour*. "Having one theme was his way to ensure this."

Timing

Churchill's bons mots are legendary. His remark about Clement Atlee, Labourite prime minister of Britain from 1945 to 1951, still stings today: "He is a modest man with much to be modest about." In fact, many of these were prepared in advance and held in reserve until the

> Facts that build the foundation for a logical conclusion are not enough. Both the audience and the speaker must be emotionally engaged.

right moment. His speeches frequently had stage directions like "pause" penciled in the margins. Montalbo notes that his dramatic pauses recaptured the attention of his audience. "Even his 'gar-rumphs' and throat clearings came at the right moment," writes Montalbo.

Visual Props

A large cigar is associated with Churchill as much as the "V-for-victory" hand gesture. Before emerging into public, he often had aides search for a "Churchill-sized" Havana. He made the bow tie and chained waistcoat part of his image. In speeches before the House of Commons, he would dramatically pull "secret" documents out of his pocket. No wonder a prominent journalist predicted in 1899 that Churchill would become "the founder of a great advertising business."

Humor

Even during England's darkest hours, Churchill leavened his speeches with humor. In one he said, "We are expecting the coming invasions; so are the fishes." On another occasion he quipped: "I get my exercise being a pallbearer for those of my friends who believed in regular running and calisthenics." The humorist and politician A. P. Herbert believed that Churchill's wit, combined with the pause, the chuckle, and "the mischievous and boyish twinkle on the face," made Churchill funnier than Noel Coward, P. G. Wodehouse, and other great British humorists of the day.

Audience Identification

In a 1943 speech at Harvard University urging harmony between the United States and Britain, he mentioned that his mother was American, making him "a child of both worlds." He borrowed from Lincoln's Second Inaugural Address in the same speech when he said: "Let us go forward with malice to none and good will to all."

Chiasmus

Chiasmus refers to a structure that repeats elements in reverse; Churchill used chiasmus to make trenchant, often witty, observations. While chancellor of the exchequer, he said, "In finance everything that is agreeable is unsound, and everything that is sound is disagreeable." He once said of the Labourite Sir Stafford Cripps, a teetotalling vegetarian: "He has all the virtues I dislike and none of the vices I admire."

Despite Churchill's skill at oratory, he was not a natural-born speaker. His stammer drove him to consult a voice specialist, who told him that it could not be corrected, but only modified. Churchill thus turned it into part of his delivery, deliberately hesitating throughout a speech. On top of this, he had a lisp. Neither was Churchill an imposing figure, his 5-foot, 8-inch frame frequently hunched over.

But he compensated for these weaknesses with a prodigious memory, a love of the English language, and a willingness to revise, revise, and revise again to capture the right combination of sense, sound, and emotion.

Reprint C0206D

Three Keys to Leadership Communication Today

• • •

Janice Obuchowski

Strategic communication has never been more important than it is today. Employees expect to know about their company's plans, and they assume that they'll participate in their company's growth. That means that leaders must make communication a personal priority and drive its value throughout the organization.

A recent book by Robert Mai and Alan Akerson, former vice presidents of the communications consultancy Fleishman-Hillard, tells leaders how to meet these challenges. In *The Leader as Communicator: Strategies to Build Loyalty, Focus Effort, and Spark Creativity*, Mai and Akerson argue that leadership communication is not simply a technical skill, but "the critical leadership competency for guiding organizations through conditions of heightened transition and turmoil."

Any competitive company, the authors say, has three critical goals:

- To attract and retain talent

- To maintain a steady course through transitions

- To stay at the leading edge of its industry through constant innovation and renewal

To accomplish these goals, leaders must do three key things:

1: Create a Community

First, leaders must be "community developers," fostering trust and creating a meaningful work environment. A direct approach often works well.

Take Saturn, where plant or unit managers take the time to welcome each new hire and explain the company's philosophy. Employees coming from organizations where they had never spoken one-on-one with a senior manager are pleasantly surprised by this. Such personalized face-to-face communication with employees conveys honesty and sincerity. Taking this approach is "the opposite of the 'seagull' style of leadership communications: Fly in, squawk a lot, and fly out," Mai and Akerson write.

A cohesive community requires a common understanding of corporate goals. Mai and Akerson recommend that leaders use storytelling as a way to articulate goals and convey trust. Construct plotlines that use employees as central characters, they advise, and build drama around the challenges posted by the company's chief competitors.

Transparent, honest communication is essential: when leaders communicate candidly, employees are likely to reciprocate, extending confidence back to the company. Thus the authors advise leaders to use clear, direct language and avoid euphemisms.

And because a group can't be a community without a two-way flow of communication, leaders need to cultivate their listening skills.

2: Steer a Steady Course

Second, leaders should act as "navigators," setting direction and instigating action, particularly during times of transition.

When MidAmerican Energy Company became aware of the trend toward deregulation, it realized it would need to educate its workforce about the changing competitive landscape. Previously the company had had a virtual monopoly over gas and electricity; now it would need to fight to win and keep customers.

> Explaining company objectives isn't enough. To persuade employees to act, leaders have to foster empathy for organizational challenges.

At the annual meeting, the company's leaders met in groups to discuss the organization's future, stimulated by worksheets that provided them with information about deregulation across other industries, statistics, and possible new company configurations. The sessions were animated, with people heatedly debating strategy and direction. After the meeting, leaders took the worksheets and held similar meetings of their own within their individual divisions.

In this manner, virtually everyone in the company participated in the same process, which yielded company-wide insight into the changing business climate and the need to take action.

Navigating is a three-step process. First, a leader needs to get people's attention. Then she needs to set clear direction. Finally, she has to persuade employees to act. To do so, she needs to foster empathy for organizational challenges. Explaining company objectives isn't enough— she needs to lay out the reasons for them and take into account employees' responses to proposed changes. What more do they want to know? What are their concerns? How can she be empathetic to their needs?

3: Commit to Continual Renewal

Third, leaders should be "renewal champions," creating an environment in which debate is normal and beneficial. Employees should feel that they can speak up and be heard; they need to know that their ideas are valued.

For instance, at Emerson, a global manufacturing company, leaders place a high priority on what the authors call "healthy conversation." Several years ago, the company decided to eliminate some employee benefits, among them a component in the employees' pre-retirement insurance program. But when an employee called the CEO directly to argue that the action was ill-considered, the CEO decided to reassess the decision.

A company in which employees feel comfortable engaging in productive conversations and sharing what they know will encounter greater success in the marketplace, the authors contend.

Finally, advise Mai and Akerson, remember that how and what you communicate will be scrutinized. The authors cite a CEO who seemed to know the names of almost all his 5,000 employees. While consulting for his organization, they saw him approach a new secretary to introduce himself. A week later, the secretary received a personal note from him wishing her good luck in her new job. The note was passed around the company, spreading goodwill.

The authors contrast this CEO with one at another company. Upset with employee work habits, he e-mailed a threatening memo to managers, outlining the punitive measures he would take if performance didn't improve. First his memo was passed around the company, and then it received an even wider audience: it was posted on Yahoo! and ultimately made the front page of the *New York Times*' business section.

The message to take away from such an incident?

"Write everything as if it might end up in the *New York Times*," write Mai and Akerson. "Because it just might."

Reprint C0404D

About the Contributors

Walter Kiechel is editor-at-large for HBS Publishing.

Loren Gary is editor of Newsletters at HBS Publishing.

Robert Kaplan is coauthor with David Norton of *Strategy Maps: Converting Intangible Assets into Tangible Outcomes* (HBS Press, 2003).

John Hintze writes about business and financial news from New York City.

David Stauffer is a contributor to *Harvard Management Update*.

Lauren Keller Johnson is a contributor to *Harvard Management Update*.

Eric McNulty is a contributor to *Harvard Management Update*.

Jennifer McFarland is a contributor to *Harvard Management Update*.

Paul Michelman is editor of *Harvard Management Update*.

Robert B. Cialdini is Regent's Professor of Psychology at Arizona State University, and author of the classic book, *Influence: Science and Practice* (Allyn & Bacon, 2001).

Nick Wreden is a consultant based in Atlanta.

Janice Obuchowski is a contributor to *Harvard Management Update*.

Harvard Business Review Paperback Series

The Harvard Business Review Paperback Series offers the best thinking on cutting-edge management ideas from the world's leading thinkers, researchers, and managers. Designed for leaders who believe in the power of ideas to change business, these books will be useful to managers at all levels of experience, but especially senior executives and general managers. In addition, this series is widely used in training and executive development programs.

Books are priced at $19.95 U.S.
Price subject to change.

Title	Product #
Harvard Business Review **Interviews with CEOs**	3294
Harvard Business Review on **Advances in Strategy**	8032
Harvard Business Review on **Appraising Employee Performance**	7685
Harvard Business Review on **Becoming a High Performance Manager**	1296
Harvard Business Review on **Brand Management**	1445
Harvard Business Review on **Breakthrough Leadership**	8059
Harvard Business Review on **Breakthrough Thinking**	181X
Harvard Business Review on **Building Personal and Organizational Resilience**	2721
Harvard Business Review on **Business and the Environment**	2336
Harvard Business Review on **The Business Value of IT**	9121
Harvard Business Review on **Change**	8842
Harvard Business Review on **Compensation**	701X
Harvard Business Review on **Corporate Ethics**	273X
Harvard Business Review on **Corporate Governance**	2379
Harvard Business Review on **Corporate Responsibility**	2748
Harvard Business Review on **Corporate Strategy**	1429
Harvard Business Review on **Crisis Management**	2352
Harvard Business Review on **Culture and Change**	8369
Harvard Business Review on **Customer Relationship Management**	6994

Title	Product #
Harvard Business Review on **Decision Making**	5572
Harvard Business Review on **Developing Leaders**	5003
Harvard Business Review on **Doing Business in China**	6387
Harvard Business Review on **Effective Communication**	1437
Harvard Business Review on **Entrepreneurship**	9105
Harvard Business Review on **Finding and Keeping the Best People**	5564
Harvard Business Review on **Innovation**	6145
Harvard Business Review on **Knowledge Management**	8818
Harvard Business Review on **Leadership**	8834
Harvard Business Review on **Leadership at the Top**	2756
Harvard Business Review on **Leading in Turbulent Times**	1806
Harvard Business Review on **Managing Diversity**	7001
Harvard Business Review on **Managing High-Tech Industries**	1828
Harvard Business Review on **Managing People**	9075
Harvard Business Review on **Managing Projects**	6395
Harvard Business Review on **Managing the Value Chain**	2344
Harvard Business Review on **Managing Uncertainty**	9083
Harvard Business Review on **Managing Your Career**	1318
Harvard Business Review on **Marketing**	8040
Harvard Business Review on **Measuring Corporate Performance**	8826
Harvard Business Review on **Mergers and Acquisitions**	5556
Harvard Business Review on **The Mind of the Leader**	6409
Harvard Business Review on **Motivating People**	1326
Harvard Business Review on **Negotiation**	2360
Harvard Business Review on **Nonprofits**	9091
Harvard Business Review on **Organizational Learning**	6153
Harvard Business Review on **Strategic Alliances**	1334
Harvard Business Review on **Strategies for Growth**	8850
Harvard Business Review on **Teams That Succeed**	502X
Harvard Business Review on **Turnarounds**	6366
Harvard Business Review on **What Makes a Leader**	6374
Harvard Business Review on **Work and Life Balance**	3286

Management Dilemmas:
Case Studies from the Pages of
Harvard Business Review

How often do you wish you could turn to a panel of experts to guide you through tough management situations? The Management Dilemmas series provides just that. Drawn from the pages of *Harvard Business Review*, each insightful volume poses several perplexing predicaments and shares the problem-solving wisdom of leading experts. Engagingly written, these solutions-oriented collections help managers make sound judgment calls when addressing everyday management dilemmas.

These books are priced at $19.95 U.S.
Price subject to change.

Title	Product #
Management Dilemmas: **When Change Comes Undone**	5038
Management Dilemmas: **When Good People Behave Badly**	5046
Management Dilemmas: **When Marketing Becomes a Minefield**	290X
Management Dilemmas: **When People Are the Problem**	7138
Management Dilemmas: **When Your Strategy Stalls**	712X

Harvard Business Essentials

In the fast-paced world of business today, everyone needs a personal resource—a place to go for advice, coaching, background information, or answers. The Harvard Business Essentials series fits the bill. Concise and straightforward, these books provide highly practical advice for readers at all levels of experience. Whether you are a new manager interested in expa\nding your skills or an experienced executive looking to stay on top, these solution-oriented books give you the reliable tips and tools you need to improve your performance and get the job done. Harvard Business Essentials titles will quickly become your constant companions and trusted guides.

These books are priced at $19.95 U.S., except as noted.
Price subject to change.

Title	Product #
Harvard Business Essentials: **Negotiation**	1113
Harvard Business Essentials: **Managing Creativity and Innovation**	1121
Harvard Business Essentials: **Managing Change and Transition**	8741
Harvard Business Essentials: **Hiring and Keeping the Best People**	875X
Harvard Business Essentials: **Finance for Managers**	8768
Harvard Business Essentials: **Business Communication**	113X
Harvard Business Essentials: **Manager's Toolkit ($24.95)**	2896
Harvard Business Essentials: **Managing Projects Large and Small**	3213
Harvard Business Essentials: **Creating Teams with an Edge**	290X
Harvard Business Essentials: **Entrepreneur's Toolkit**	4368
Harvard Business Essentials: **Coaching and Mentoring**	435X
Harvard Business Essentials: **Crisis Management**	4376

The Results-Driven Manager

The Results-Driven Manager series collects timely articles from *Harvard Management Update* and *Harvard Management Communication Letter* to help senior to middle managers sharpen their skills, increase their effectiveness, and gain a competitive edge. Presented in a concise, accessible format to save managers valuable time, these books offer authoritative insights and techniques for improving job performance and achieving immediate results.

These books are priced at $14.95 U.S.
Price subject to change.

Title	Product #
The Results-Driven Manager: **Face-to-Face Communications for Clarity and Impact**	3477
The Results-Driven Manager: **Managing Yourself for the Career You Want**	3469
The Results-Driven Manager: **Presentations That Persuade and Motivate**	3493
The Results-Driven Manager: **Teams That Click**	3507
The Results-Driven Manager: **Winning Negotiations That Preserve Relationships**	3485
The Results-Driven Manager: **Dealing with Difficult People**	6344
The Results-Driven Manager: **Taking Control of Your Time**	6352
The Results-Driven Manager: **Getting People on Board**	6360
The Results-Driven Manager: **Motivating People for Improved Performance**	7790
The Results-Driven Manager: **Becoming an Effective Leader**	7804
The Results-Driven Manager: **Managing Change to Reduce Resistance**	7812

How to Order

Harvard Business School Press publications are available worldwide from your local bookseller or online retailer.
You can also call

1-800-668-6780

Our product consultants are available to help you
8:00 a.m.–6:00 p.m., Monday–Friday, Eastern Time.
Outside the U.S. and Canada, call: 617-783-7450
Please call about special discounts for quantities greater than ten.

You can order online at

www.HBSPress.org